THE LETTER CODE

DECIPHERING WHY YOU LOVE THE WAY YOU LOVE

Krystal J. White, Ph.D.

Executive Shaman Publishing

The names and some of the identifying details of the people mentioned in the book have been changed to protect their privacy. In some cases, the stories are composites of several people.

Executive Shaman Publishing
www.theexecutiveshaman.com
krystal@theexecutiveshaman.com

Editing and production by Stephanie Gunning
Cover design by Gus Yoo
Illustrations by Eva Isabel Us
Book Layout © Book Design Templates

Ordering Information:
Quantity sales. Special discounts are available on quantity purchases by corporations, associations, and others. For details, contact the publisher at the email address above.

Library of Congress Control Number 2019900012

The Letter Code/Krystal J. White —1st ed.
ISBN 978-1-7335032-0-4 (paperback)

Dedication

To you, the one who flipped open to this page of the book, curious enough to give it your precious attention. To the willing one. To the one who seeks. To the one that does not need to seek, and yet finds himself here anyway. To the one who won't go further, and the one that must return again. To the one connected to me right now, right here. This is it. Whoever you are, no matter why you're here, trust that this—all of this—is for you.

Contents

AUTHOR'S NOTE

Many terms can be used for individuals in couples, whether they are in serious relationships or only just beginning to intentionally develop one. Most of the time, I chose to use as neutral and inclusive a term as possible, usually *significant other* or *partner*. Our culture is curiously questioning our traditional use of language. We are at a time of becoming more aware of how powerfully influential our words are. What we call ourselves matters more now than it did in previous decades. This book is intended to guide individuals who genuinely want a significant, thriving, and romantic connection with another person who is their "person." The designation for this relationship can be short-lived or last a lifetime. It's up to you to determine where you are at, and if your intention is building, sustaining or revitalizing significant connectivity. The terms by which I refer to partners in this book could apply to married people, people in legal partnerships, routine lovers, boyfriends, girlfriends, and even friends "with benefits."

When speaking in generalities about relational roles, I will sometimes refer to a significant partner as *him* and sometimes as *her*. I do not assume that either is more accurate. Nor do I believe that *partner* or *significant other* are your preferred terms for "your person." Although I have more questions about these terms than answers, I feel (mostly) comfortable working within these linguistic limitations.

If the terms *partner* or *significant other* don't work for you, please substitute the term that works for you in their place as you are reading.

THE DECODER

Every warrior lives by a code. And every lover loves by one.

Although it is often hidden, we all have a personal code that explains who we are at our core, what values we fight for, and why we love the way we love.

People construct codes to keep secrets hidden, classify information, and consolidate learning. We also break codes to unearth essential truths, deconstruct the world we encounter, and expand our understanding. Codes are engrained in every part of our culture, from communication and commerce, to politics, psychology, warfare, and entertainment. Learning the codes that underlie our behavior enables us to master any circumstance. Loving by them enables us to be powerfully connected.

This book is about deciphering yours.

Seeing Beyond the Surface

I've been a decoder for most of my life. As a child in the early 1980s, I was obsessed with the toy rings that came as prizes in cereal boxes in the early 1980s. As I grew up, I abandoned these simple ciphers in favor of more sophisticated tools, techniques, and systems. Magnifying glasses gave way to microscopes and a fascination with the periodic table of elements flowed into an affinity for molecular biology. My admiration of science subsequently blossomed into multiple graduate studies in in philosophy, theology, and psychology.

As a leadership psychologist, my role involves pinpointing and strategically revealing what drives human behavior. The multidisciplinary training and professional experiences I've accumulated equip me to see what is often unseen. Revealing what is forgotten, lost, buried, hidden, or obscured often is the key needed to shift from problem to solution. When people experience an "aha moment" and understand their own codes, change naturally follows.

It is clear that we haven't entirely cracked the code of the human heart. Most of us cannot see what lies beyond the surface of our romantic endeavors. Just as warriors rely on effective and powerful weapons to fight fairly, lovers need resources in order to love fully. Too often, these tools aren't easily available. If all is *to be* fair in love and war, we need more powerful weapons in the name of love. The Letter Code system was devised for this purpose.

This Isn't Working

A stranger and I once chatted about life, liberty, and love while traveling on a high-speed train from Paris to Frankfurt. Eventually, he confessed to me that he was disappointed and frustrated that he couldn't figure out how to bring life back into his marriage. The fit just wasn't right, and he wanted simple advice on what to do about it. Throughout our discussion, I found myself absolutely intrigued by the fact that this man—attractive, empathetic, and successful in every other area of his life—didn't feel fulfilled in his love life. I resonated with his predicament, although our lives were extremely different. Despite not being married for more than two decades, I still distinctly remembered what it felt like to be out of internal alignment in my marriage, and externally disconnected from my partner.

Wrestling with the decision to divorce was more challenging than any degree I had earned or mountain I had summitted. My ex-husband and I made sincere efforts to repair the connection, including extensive individual and couples counseling. But our brief marriage *just didn't work*. Knowing what we wanted and working hard to try to get it only kept us stuck. We divorced with a lot of pain.

In a day and age where information is at our fingertips and a powerful Wi-Fi connection is an important requirement in our dwellings and workplaces, many of us nonetheless feel disconnected, stagnant, misunderstood, lost, and resigned when it comes love. If you've sometimes wondered if you're cut out for a long-term relationship, you're not alone. If you've been wanting to change something about how you typically relate, you're not alone. If you find relationship advice too complicated and convoluted to effectively implement, you're not alone.

The Codes of Love

Despite my being a decoder professionally, I could not discern my love code, no matter how much I achieved or explored. For years, I made the same mistakes over and over in my relationships, chasing the same misguided ideals over and over. When the dynamics of sustaining an authentic, fulfilling love connection became too cryptic and too complicated, I had my own "aha moment." Just like in all the other areas of my life, I realized there must be a simpler explanation of why I love the way I love.

The Letter Code system emerged soon after this realization, during a once-in-a-lifetime hiking tour of Patagonia. A series of vulnerable conversations with fellow backpackers, strangers when we met, sparked in my mind the notion of codes. If we live by codes, we must love by them, too. As oxygen was given to this originally vague idea, its flames quickly grew into a functional, easy-to-use system. Just as tribes and clans display their code on a totem pole or coat of arms, simple letters can visually depict our love codes. Each one simply signifies the different things we unconsciously seek from love.

For the past two years, each time I mentioned the Letter Code, others were eager to understand and use the system too. I quickly learned that most of us want to understand love better. We just need it to be easy.

Four Foundations

The truth is that we all are primarily driven by one of four factors when it comes to love. Four is the spiritual number of stability and one's innermost foundation. As people, we are complicated and diverse on the surface, demonstrating a range of desires, talents, skills, and preferences. Our demographics, personalities, life experiences, and circumstances may vary widely, but internally, those differences diminish. Everybody's core needs are similar, and there are only a few basic core psychological needs that define us in love. Once we know our key motivation, it becomes much easier to achieve balance as an individual in a relationship. Having achieved internal balance, creating an enjoyable connection with our partner requires *a lot* less effort.

Of course, being coupled can involve a tremendous amount of questioning, compromising, and conscious hard work. Most adults discover sooner rather than later that sexual chemistry and romantic love aren't enough to help us sustain a thriving relationship in the long term. Sustained relationships require self-understanding, deliberate commitment, and taking responsibility for seeing that our own our basic needs get met.

Having needs doesn't indicate that we are dysfunctional. Rather, needs are the true source of our power as people. When our needs are met, this sets off a positive chain reaction: We stay close to our authentic self, we relax, trust deepens in our relationships, and we feel more turned on. These needs are inside of us all along, encouraging us to reach out, share ourselves, and love freely. They are the true source of belonging and acceptance.

The only problem with this paradigm is that our true needs are often hidden from us.

In this book, you will be introduced to a system designed to reveal what you need to be centered and balanced—and happy—in a relationship. No matter your past circumstances in love or what you've believed about yourself as a partner until now, there is an essential truth when it comes to being you in love. Grasping this truth will change everything! It will allow you to deliberately create, restore, and be fulfilled in ways you may never have experienced in a partnership before.

This is a book for healthy adults seeking a hack—a shortcut—for romantic compatibility. It isn't a book for people seeking an in-depth, step-by-step process for saving a troubled relationship. It's for "real" people loving in the "real" modern world. It is written for you if you want to quickly understand yourself better and don't have the time, interest, or energy to get a Ph.D. in modern love. We've all got expenses like house payments or college tuition to plan out, a Netflix or Hulu queue to get through, sisters whose birthday cards are overdue, and thirtieth, fortieth, or fiftieth birthday trips to schedule. We've all got various deadlines to meet.

The Letter Code is for men and women who are straight or gay, extroverted or introverted, married or single and seriously dating. It is not about hooking up for a one-night stand or a shot-term fling. It's for what happens after your initial attraction and lust wear off and you want emotional connectivity without it costing too much energy.

This is a relationship book for all individuals who want to understand themselves better in order to deepen the connection they have with the person they are trying to love. The four-part system it teaches provides you with a quick hack to make yourself more effective at building a bond, creating internal balance, and deepening connection.

In these pages we will solve the mystery of how some people develop amazing connectivity in their partnerships. If you're looking for a fast, efficient, and fulfilling method for understanding their secrets, this method is for you.

You've just been recruited as a decoder.

CHAPTER ONE

A LOVE HACK

"I *am not sure you know what you need."*
My boyfriend quipped this as I struggled to decide what to order for dinner. This was years ago. We were both in our early thirties and we had been dating more than six months. But this was the first time he'd said anything that approached criticism. When he said it, he wasn't only talking about my wishy-washiness over the menu. Looking more closely, it became clear that he was speaking about my hesitation to move in together. On the outside, his statement motivated me to quickly select whatever the waiter recommended. On the inside, his statement motivated me to slowly reflect on what was driving my ambivalence.

When people tell us things we don't like to hear, our tendency is to deny, rationalize, or blame. I probably did all three at the time. Now, looking back, I realize that the comment was woefully spot on. I just hadn't figured out *why*.

At the time, I could have told you a lot about myself, mostly features of myself as an individual. When it came to who I became in significant romantic relationships, however, all information I could have provided you at the time was superficial fluff. I had no true understanding of why I did what I did in romantic relationships, from moving in too soon, to breaking up prematurely or staying long past the relationship's expiration date.

Most of us have little self-awareness of what drives us in love. On the surface, we can see what we're doing wrong. We choose the wrong person, the wrong behavior, or the wrong time to get involved. We can see also what we're doing right. We choose the right person, engage in the right behavior, and we do so with perfect timing. We just don't understand why—what's at the heart of it all? Even as a psychologist, I struggle to be self-aware when it comes to romantic relationships.

Here's the bottom line up front: We don't know the true reasons we do what we do, think what we think, want what we want, and need what we need when it comes to love. And if understanding our reasons was our goal, it would take a long time spent in self-reflection or therapy, and many relationship trials, to figure them out.

Our personal letter code signifies our unrealized, underlying motivation in love. It's a hack for quickly getting what we *really* need in our intimate relationships.

Consider the following. Samantha is a fifty-year-old lawyer by training and a practicing judge, married for the last twenty-four years to her husband. On the surface, she is the primary caretaker of their single child, the primary planner of their family holidays, and the overseer of their household finances. She frequently reports to trusted others that she wants her husband to be more at home, to be less ambitious, and to put the needs of his family ahead of his career.

Samantha wasn't aware that what she really wants is more free time for herself, especially to pursue her own professional interests. She had no clue that underneath what she *says* she wants is what she *really* wants: autonomy. Changing her individual identity to create a joint lifestyle just didn't fuel her. Her complaints about what she wants more from him covered up *what she needs more of* for herself.

The Letter Code system helps us to deduce the need that is the at the root of our stated wants and genuine wants. Like knowing the root system of trees, , figuring out this core motivator quickly leads to being able to truly nourish your relationship.

Dazed and Confused

There aren't many places, programs, families, or friendships that teach us to understand ourselves well, especially when it comes to our behavior in an intimate relationship. Who really encourages us to figure ourselves out? The nitty-gritty details often go unexplored, so they are hidden and misunderstood. It's common for us not to have close friends or objective family members that will help us to see all the ways we're fooling ourselves when it comes to our love lives. We often have no idea what we are really doing, or why. Even if we do know what we are doing (for example, trying to rekindle a spark of desire or figuring out if we can make a marriage work), we often aren't encouraged by the people we know to dig deep and figure out what our essential needs are.

It's hard enough to figure out our own needs as an individual. Add in the needs of someone we love, and things quickly become more confusing. We are sometimes desperate to connect and merge, and other times we desperately want to run and have space. We experience moments of warmth, belonging, and acceptance that give us a sense of peace. And then we experience moments of misunderstanding, isolation, and judgment that give us pain. We approach, we retreat, we embrace, and we get sucker punched. Sometimes many of these moments can be experienced within the course of one week with a significant other. Love often leaves us dazed and confused. In such a state, it's easy to return to familiar patterns of behavior, even if we know that they won't lead to our fulfillment.

"We just weren't compatible."

This is one of the most common answers people give when a relationship ends. It is often *my* go-to superficial reason. We all have thoughts about being with a partner who "gets" us, and who we "just get" too. Many of us just want to naturally click together, like two pieces of Lego snapping into place. For the purposes of this book, that clicking is going to be referred to as *connectivity*. *Connectivity* is a word that describes the capability and quality of clicking between you and your significant other. Connectivity is a systemic way you and your partner exchange energy. Imagine a live wire of energy running between the two of you. Why does it sometimes feel fast, easy, and positive and other times slow, belabored, and negative?

Most of us answer these questions by stating something about our compatibility. It's the "no-fault" and "no-credit" explanation for connectivity. While some couples *appear* to share a certain degree of natural connection, most research on romantic relationships indicates that once couples get past the initial stage of lust, connectivity requires upkeep. That's hard to do, being that it is a moving, and often camouflaged target.

We often don't examine beyond the superficial blaming of compatibility as the cause of the challenges we face in our relationships. If we did, we might uncover hard to face beliefs, such as a belief that:

1. Another person was unable, unwilling, or inadequate to meet our needs.
2. We were unable, unwilling, or inadequate to meet a partner's needs.

Psychologically speaking, we are prone to adopt one or the other automatic perspective. Discussions of compatibility problems often mask what's really going on and why we love the way we love.

Compatibility does exist, but as a psychologist I can assure you that focusing on it as a goal rarely brings effective relational change. There is a way, however, to manufacture what the entire concept of compatibility aims for: fulfilling and easy-to-maintain connectivity.

It Starts with You

I wrote *The Letter Code* to help you to discover the simple root cause for why you want what you want, feel the way you feel, and act how you act in love.

Once you know this core need, you can set about creating conditions to fulfill it.

Your relational fulfillment starts with you.

Before giving responsibility for connectivity to anyone else, you must first understand your own hidden motivations. Then you can build the love that is a right fit for you from this solid foundation. This is true whether you are currently married or engaged, dating, or looking for a new significant partner.

I know my individual personality quite well. I'm extroverted, bold, romantic, and idealistic. I am aware that these traits are sometimes strengths and sometimes weaknesses. I am aware of my personal needs: I need five hours of sleep, I need significant degrees of freedom, I need deep philosophical, social, and psychological engagement with others, and I need physical activity to clear out my mental chatter. All of these are singular traits, however. They didn't help me understand what I really, truly *need* in a loving significant relationship before I deciphered my own letter code.

When our needs and beliefs about connectivity lie unexamined, our essential love lives are encoded. We can operate only according to what we see, which is not the essential truth of our being. We process information and make decisions according to fast interpretations. These assumptions fail to speak genuinely to the underlying needs that are waiting to be fulfilled beneath the surface of our awareness. We can feel starved if hidden needs are unmet.

Fast-Food Love

Of course, life today moves quickly. Who has time to look at all the details? The weight of our responsibilities is real. Our Outlook, Gmail, and Facebook accounts demand our attention. Time marches on, and we want to move on with it.

We live in a world where we have limited time to figure ourselves out. Research from multiple scientific fields demonstrates that the human brain, identity, and value system each take over twenty years to fully develop. Who we are as individuals isn't solidified by the time most of us start our love lives in our teens and twenties. We want to please, perform well, and feel good about ourselves in the meantime. By the time we've experienced the beginnings and endings of a few significant relationships with similarly inexperienced lovers, we can be confused. The lesson many of us choose to take from these relationships is what we want less of, more of, or the same amount of (just expressed differently) in the other person.

Some of us may attempt to learn how we can change ourselves as a result of our previous significant relationship lessons. Others of us start playing by someone else's set of rules, alter our approaches to getting what (we think) we want, or develop various identities, roles, and "hats" we can wear just to get through the date, the wedding, the relocations, the child-rearing, and the family holiday celebration that occur during our lifetimes.

Do you really know what your core needs in love are? Before discerning my letter code, I didn't know mine.

In my opinion, if we're lucky to have significant support, others that know us well, they may tell us what we need. But often, they are only reflecting *their own needs back to us.* Figuring out what we truly need requires slowing down, genuinely asking, and really answering, some key questions, and making choices that honor the truth.

When we become more aware of how we hide our needs, we can see more clearly how to prevent our relationships from becoming misaligned, overtaxed, and poorly resourced. We can switch from disguising them to revealing them. From fast-food connection to true nourishment.

Don't get me wrong, even if we allow ourselves to get away with being superficial, we can be successful in most areas of our lives. Happy even. We can be competent and committed leaders, bosses, parents, and friends if we're revealing only our surface selves. But there is one area of our lives where this is not enough to satisfy us: our love lives.

Imagine how much more fulfilling your love life would be if you understood yourself and your needs even a small fraction better and were brave enough to be genuine in getting them met.

In the chapters that follow, I'm going to teach you a quick, short-hand method for discerning your authentic motivations. This information is going to raise your love IQ and provide you with a foundation to create deep connectivity with your partner that flows naturally between you. That connection won't feel superficial or phony. It will feel genuine and fueling.

Exploring what's below the surface, what our hearts truly are saying, is worth these benefits. *The Letter Code* gives you an easy way to get to the heart of the matter, to discover why you love the way you love.

CHAPTER TWO

REVEALING THE REAL YOU IN LOVE

You know the feeling of being completely yourself, unencumbered and free. It feels like a peaceful contentment. We all want relationships, especially romantic partnerships, where we can be intimately and positively connected to our significant others and be our true selves at the same time. We need to find our own centers to achieve this dynamic. Feeling successful in our relationships is reliant on our ability to uncover and respond to our hidden core love needs.

If you're like me, you live in a complicated world and find yourself to be rather complicated, too. Being "authentic" is not as easy as it sounds. You need to shift through lots of detail on the surface to quickly get to the simple, real you underneath all the roles, responsibilities, and rules you have adopted. Your letter code is a hack for deciphering all this superficial stuff to get to the most essential way you genuinely connect with your significant others.

Your letter code reveals the basic need you are seeking to fulfill in love—and have been all your life—although you may not have known it. It dictates how you fundamentally relate to your romantic partners and explains the reason why. Everybody has a combination of needs that, when met, facilitate them in clicking with their partner. The love connection just flows when this occurs.

You know this clicking when you feel it. It happens when you are loving from your real code and not a false one. Staying close to your code— your real center of love—will quickly reduce how much effort you put forth to connect, and it will increase your experience of being in the right place to feel love.

In this book, you will be guided to classify your behavior, feelings, and thoughts into their most essential form. Knowing our codes helps us quickly translate and communicate our real selves to the significant others we'd like to love better.

People have only one of four main romantic love profiles that explains their patterns of connectivity. The needs that underlie each of these profiles are recognizable and easy to understand. The four letter codes represent essential patterns of thought, feeling, and actions. These are expressed in how emotionally close or distant people like to be in relationship with their significant others. They also help us decipher the degree to which we seek either autonomy or support from them.

Under different circumstances, some people need either to move emotionally closer to their partners or emotionally away from their partners. Other people don't need to move at all, needing instead to remain grounded, while either standing together or standing apart. Each of these four behavioral styles conveys how people achieve connectivity with their significant others.

In this book, I'm giving you a quick tool for understanding the four main types of psychological needs driving how we love. Without psychobabble or spending time trying to deduce the origins of your profile, I'm going to give you quick, user-friendly information on how much support, togetherness, groundedness, and separation you naturally need in your love life to click with a partner.

How to feel fulfilled, happy, and aligned with a significant other may have been hidden to you up to now. But I want you to be able to see the real you in love. Knowing your letter code has the potential to powerfully change the way you love from here on out.

You Get the Picture

Consider the body language when two people approach one another in greeting. Some people lean in, some people stand upright, and some lean away. Some people even want to be so close that they are practically standing on top of one another. These physical patterns are like the lines making up letters in an alphabet. Imagine that each person's body is a straight line. Lines join together to make a letter, just as two adults connect together to form a couple. Being able to read the letters is a hack that can help you quickly understand yourself.

It is not possible to accurately discern anybody's relationship needs purely from observing the way he or she approaches others. What you see is *not* what you get. But you can decipher *your own core* needs in a relationship by examining what's beneath your patterns of feeling, thinking, wanting, and behaving in love.

The reason to do this is because you can't change what you can't see. Once you can see your letter code, you'll be more effective in connecting with others while being the real you.

The Different Ways We Touch

Looking at how the lines of our energy and behavior touch and connect reveals commonalities and differences in our core needs in relationship.

LEANING IN

Some people need to lean into a relationship, wanting to establish a mutually supportive connection. If this feels right for you, you want not only to assist your partner, but to also lift her up emotionally. You want both of you to be there to help each other when vulnerable and receive a significant degree of support from the connection. Without this consistent support, you will feel that something just isn't right. You may feel slight unease, disappointment, or frustration—perhaps assuming that you are being taken for granted or mistreated. Or you could feel self-judgmental, becoming dissatisfied with yourself for not being enough or doing well enough to have earned and received the support you wanted.

You may be a person who naturally needs a significant degree of emotional vulnerability. You appreciate it when you are needed; and if you are being honest with yourself, you like it when you can trust it is safe for you to need someone. Getting this need met provides you with an essential sense of stability.

LEANING BACK

Some people need to lean back from a relationship, wanting to diverge from their significant others. If this sounds like you, there are times when you will seek to go into a completely different direction from your significant other. You need periodic diversion from being a couple in order to feel satisfied. Leaning away occasionally, or even frequently, gives you space to reflect on your own life, to feel more gratitude for the relationship, and to bring vitality and renewed passion back to your relationship.

If your partner does not like or genuinely value this type of leaning away, you may feel frustrated, ashamed, or guilty of your desire. You may establish destructive habits to gain this freedom or to repress your need for it. Neither is an ideal solution. By contrast, if you can lovingly express your need to have separate experiences and your partner is willing to embrace your need, as a couple you may discover that adventures external to your partnership actually brings integrity to the relationship.

STANDING SIDE BY SIDE

Some people feel a need to be grounded and upright. They prefer to touch in ways where each person isn't required to lean in to connect. They prefer to stand side by side in love. If this sounds like you, you tend to find purpose in maintaining a solid, rooted foundation. You feel fulfilled by being steadfast in your commitments, and you value a strong work ethic. You view relationships as partnerships where two people care about each other's wellbeing and take responsibility for themselves as well. It feels important to you to see eye to eye with your partner and to function as equals.

REACHING OUT

Some people are looking for companionship from their significant others. Companionship provides a bridge of connection between otherwise separate entities. If you deeply appreciate it when your partner reaches out to you in reciprocity to enjoy common interests, tasks/projects, activities, and experiences, this may be your preferred dynamic. Sharing and collaborating is a link to your significant other that provides a clear way for you to enhance your mutual pleasure.

Focus on Yourself First

In the next four chapters, you're going to learn how to decipher your personal letter code and hidden relationship needs. It doesn't matter if you are in a long-term relationship, such as a marriage, or if you are only casually dating right now. In either case, you have built-in, natural ways of joining your life with a person you genuinely want to love. Once you know your core need and can more easily see it behind your thoughts, emotions, and actions, then you can start to build (or rebuild) your love life from a foundation of empowered awareness rather than false interpretations.

Each letter code visually represents the type of relationship a person is either consciously or unconsciously trying to create according to his or her personal motivation. Understand your letter code and you'll be clued in about your innermost need.

Beware! Trying to guess your significant other's letter code could lead to disconnection. Remember, these needs are mostly hidden from us. We can spend many years superficially reading our relationships one way, while the truth of what we need is completely the opposite. You'll get much better results if you work on deciphering your own motivation first before you try to guide your significant partner to decode his/her own needs.

Focus on yourself. That often serves as a powerful tool to influence others to do the same.

CHAPTER THREE

WHY YOU LOVE THE WAY YOU LOVE

It's time for you to see yourself as a partner more fully. If we only see our surface selves, we risk only seeing the surface of others.

Refusing to assume that what is superficial is true serves as the cornerstone of conscious problem solving. If our aim is enhanced connectivity with our significant others, we must understand ourselves deeply *and* demonstrate our desire to deeply understand our significant others.

Discovering your letter code is the first step.

Are you ready?

The Letter Code Test

You'll need twenty to thirty minutes, a timer, and writing materials to do the four exercises in this self-assessment.

EXERCISE 1: QUICK-FIRE RESPONSES

In a moment, I will ask you to answer four questions. Set the timer to one minute for each question and use the entire minute to write your response. Prior to writing, do not think, reflect, or edit yourself. Just write down your automatic impressions.

1. What do I think real love with another individual is truly about?

2. What do I naturally bring or contribute to a significant relationship?

3. What do I want from my most significant relationship?

4. In my significant relationship, when do I feel most satisfied, stable, and fulfilled?

EXERCISE 2: CORE TRUTH RESPONSES

Now, I will ask you to answer the same four questions again, encouraging you to dig deeper than your first responses. This time add on what may be more difficult to see at the surface level and remove what is a façade. Go beyond messages you've seen in the media and what you've heard other people say or write about relationships. Edit what you think your current or past partners have wanted you to be and focus on your own core truth.

Set the timer for three minutes for each question. Take the entire three minutes to write down your responses. If you run out of something to say, that's okay. Just sit there and catch the next thought that comes up. Don't rush ahead. Deeper, more authentic responses sometimes follow initial, automatic responses. Although the time may feel like a *long* time, many people report that it is during the last thirty seconds of responding to a question that their most genuine responses come through. Resist the urge to end the exercise early. Just keep asking yourself *What else? Anything else?*

1. What do I think real love with another individual is truly about?

2. What do I naturally bring or contribute to a significant relationship?

3. What do I want from my most significant relationship?

4. In my significant relationship, when do I feel most satisfied, stable, and fulfilled?

You should notice that your responses became more genuine, deeper, and more focused than they were in Exercise 1.

EXERCISE 3: PRIORITIZING YOUR NATURAL PREFERENCES

Most adults have learned how to accommodate themselves to the environments they are in. We often live, work, study, play, and parent in situations that take more energy from us than they provide. Relationships are no different. If you understand *and prioritize* your preferences, you can design a better environment where the energy-suck of accommodation is rarely necessary.

Take the next ten minutes to answer the following seven multiple-choice questions. Select the choice in each set that best represents you currently, as your "real" self. By this, I mean the version of you that emerges when you're not trying to perform for or appease anyone else. Try also to think of who you would be without the influence of convention—without trying to match what you think you *should be* or acting in the ways that your partner is suggesting that you should.

You will most likely be pulled to choose more than one response. That's normal. If you feel conflicted, simply rank each response from most to least like you. When you have trouble deciding the order, ask yourself: What comes first? What is my highest priority? What is the *most* important of them all? Then, circle your top choice.

Begin.

1. **You naturally feel energized (although you may not always like it) when:**
   A. Your partner is pursuing a respectable goal.
   B. Your partner nurtures and builds you up.
   C. Your partner joins forces with you in complete devotion.
   D. Your partner challenges you.

2. **You naturally lose energy (but may not always notice it) when:**
   A. Your partner constantly checks in on you.
   B. Your partner doesn't recognize your efforts to care for him/her.
   C. Your partner is unresponsive or disengaged with you in some way.
   D. Your partner is resistant or slow to change.

3. **You secretly fear that:**
   A. Your partner needs you more than you need him/her.
   B. You are unable to give as much as you'd like to your partner.
   C. You and your partner are not on the same level in many ways.
   D. You or your partner won't seize opportunities to grow.

4. **You find yourself saying about significant relationships that:**
   A. Each person needs to have his/her own life.
   B. Each person should put the other's needs ahead of his/her own.
   C. You should marry your best friend.
   D. Each person should be growing as an individual because of the relationship.

5. **You prefer it when your significant other:**
   A. Actively participates in his/her own interests, hobbies, and aspirations.
   B. Does things intended to make you feel good without needing to be asked.
   C. Actively participates with you in your interests, hobbies, and aspirations.
   D. Actively participates in experiences or activities designed for his/her self-improvement.

6. **To feel stable and secure in a relationship, you prefer:**
   A. To be in control of your own life.
   B. To feel that you are needed and accepted when you need something.
   C. To join your life with your partner's, so you are building a team.
   D. It when there is forward momentum and progression.

7. **Emotionally, you primarily connect with your partner through:**
   A. Sharing your time, home, body, and/or projects.
   B. Mutual caretaking activities and companionship.
   C. Sustaining a united lifestyle, where most of your experiences, thoughts, and feelings are aligned.
   D. Influencing each other to improve.

This concludes the question-and-answer portion of this exercise. Below, next to each letter, tally the number of times you ranked that letter as your number one priority. Circle the letter with the highest score.

A _____   B _____   C _____   D _____

Using the key below, now change your highest score letter into its decoded letter equivalent.

A ➜ H

B ➜ A

C ➜ Y

D ➜ W

EXERCISE 4: CONFIRM YOUR RESULTS

Decoders typically double check their answers before reporting their results. Based on the insights you developed by doing Exercises 1, 2, and 3, review the following four descriptions of the letter codes A, Y, W, and H (see pages 41–42). Look for words, phrases, intentions, and images that are like the discoveries you made in your writing about yourself. Compare them with your multiple-choice letter selection.

Now, select the letter code that is the best fit with your responses across all exercises. If you have any difficulty making your selection, ask yourself this question: *During intense conflicts that have occurred in my current or a past relationship, what essential need did I have that was not being met?*

Be careful to choose the letter code that represents the most genuine you. Who are you when it's just you in the room you're in?

A

Your most essential need is for mutual support.

You naturally nurture others and appreciate it when they are kind to you.

You value the perspectives and experiences of others and seek to understand them.

You believe that love should be kind, patient, and accommodating.

When your partner has a problem, you want to be able to uplift him/her.

You want to be accepted for who you naturally are.

W

Your most essential need is for growth.

You appreciate it when your partner questions or challenges you.

You like to motivate your significant other to improve.

You often seek experiences that stretch you outside your comfort zone.

You prefer change and stimulation compared to routine.

You are equally heart strong and headstrong.

H

Your most essential need is for independence.

You desire an equal partner, someone self-reliant who carries his/her own weight.

You show love through companionship.

You value being respected for doing an excellent job.

You want to be desired rather than needed.

You seek to maintain a strong sense of self.

No matter how good your relationship is, you need time on your own.

Y

Your most essential need is for unity.

You naturally collaborate and like to make decisions jointly.

You value teamwork and acts of solidarity.

You like to know what's going on in every area of your significant other's life.

You believe love should provide stability.

You believe that if one partner fails, the other also fails.

You naturally want your significant other to be your best friend.

***

Now you know your personal letter code!

You can turn directly now to the chapter describing your code—to verify it—or read all the chapters in sequence to gain a fuller understanding of the key drivers in love.

If you believe you're an H, turn to page 45.

If you believe you're an A, turn to page73.

If you believe you're a Y, turn to page 101.

If you believe you're a W, turn to page 129.

CHAPTER FOUR

LETTER H

I n order to feel fulfilled in their significant relationships, Hs need independence.

Hs are people who have established their own definitive stances in the world; and they need this in their intimate relationships as well. Hs dance to the sound of their own drums, play their own tunes, and, most likely, consider themselves unconventional in some areas of their lives. They are firmly planted in strong psychological foundations and do not *need* a partner to provide them with emotional fulfillment or stability, or to inform their sense of identity. They *want* to find a person with whom to establish a steady, strong romantic connection that offers a shared purpose. At the same time, they need their romantic partner to respect their need for independence.

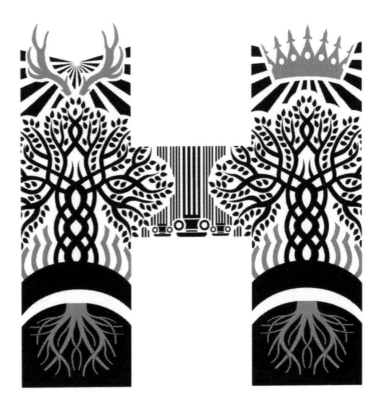

The shape of the H demonstrates two people independently standing across from each other another, sharing a strong tie that connects them. Individuals who are Hs neither lean toward or away from their person. They stand upright and see eye to eye with their significant others. They want an intimate partner, but do not need one for balance. Emotional independence in this connectivity dynamic brings Hs immense fulfillment.

If you are an H, most likely you can relate to these descriptions. Using your letter code, it becomes easy to discern what you need out of a serious, romantic partnership: to love while maintaining your individuality. You achieve a sense of stability from being emotionally self-sufficient but also lovingly connected.

You are driven to successfully stand on your own two feet and maintain your own foundation. Your relationship provides pleasure and satisfaction from companionship with your partner. As an H, you want to share something with your partner that can serve as a bridge between the two of you. That "bridge" ideally serves a communal function. It may be to create a home base, raise children or animals together, study together, collaborate on projects, train for an athletic event together, or simply enjoy mundane activities together.

Hs want connectivity. But they won't feel comfortable in relationships that threaten to destabilize them. They are the type of individuals that genuinely need to remain somewhat separate, because they are steadier that way. Hs that thrive in love learn how to be autonomous without it leading to isolation. They prefer to maintain connectivity that serves the wellbeing of each separate individual.

As an H, you can connect in meaningful ways, even across long, impressive distances. You often see the bigger picture and desire your partner to achieve his or her individual goals. You resonate with the idea of being a "power couple," each successful and competent in his or her own domain. Although a romantic partnership isn't required to give you emotional support, it can provide you with a significant amount of satisfaction. (If support is what you need, skip to the next chapter, as you might not be an H.) Emotionally speaking, a dependable and trustworthy partner gives a you a sense of joy, relief, and bigger purpose. You like being self-sufficient, but you also like it when your relationship gives you something "extra." You may find that you typically approach a relationship like you would eating dinner. Love is not the main course, but that doesn't mean you don't fully desire and appreciate dessert.

What do Hs want? To create and share a connection to something more meaningful, pleasurable, effective, or efficient than they can achieve on their own. The relationship is not the end-all of the H existence; it is one out of many means to attain life satisfaction.

Your average H wants a relationship to honor individual routines, traditions, and aspirations. For the H to be satisfied, the H needs to feel respected in his or her own pursuits. Many Hs tend not to crave or pine after a relationship if they aren't in one. Once a romantic commitment has been established, however, what that specific relationship adds to his or her life matters to an H. Hs are unlikely to dissolve a relationship if they feel the relationship is effectively serving this role.

Hs need to have a relationship that brings out the best in both parties. They know, love, and lead themselves and often expect or influence others to do the same. Hs naturally learn from their partners' skills and talents, and like it when their partners have their own ambition and goals. They may secretly crave a partner who is his own hero and is prosocial and proactive.

Key Qualities of an H in Love

Hs are in love when the relationship has positive connectivity that aligns with their natural need for independence. When this occurs, they naturally demonstrate:

- **Stability.** Hs will maintain their strategy and priorities despite what's going on in a relationship. This is the partner who, after staying up all night having sex or deciding to break up, will still show up to work. Hs will follow through on their plans for the day despite unexpected relational joys or pains.
- **Honesty.** Hs are the type of lovers who actually want to be able to discuss all factors of the relationship and can be quite blunt in how they communicate. If a partner asks an H her opinion or perspective, an H will feel compelled to share her truth and the logic behind what she shared. On the flip side, Hs

adore hearing straightforward, no bullshit truth from their significant others, and they are not afraid of conflict or criticism.

- **Self-reliance.** Hs will try to do something on their own before asking for help. When a partner texts them to ask how their day was, an H may share that she had an awful morning, her tire blew out on the highway, and it took an extra hour to take care of it. Most of the time, Hs will tell you what occurred after the problem is solved.

- **Rationality.** Hs often have a set of criteria that they like to see their partners, or their partnerships, possess. These standards are defined by the H, not by society. And Hs are likely able to list their top values when asked (they may even have them written down somewhere). If an H wants to start a new romance or improve one that is not meeting their standards, they will come up with a concrete, logical strategy for how to do so.

- **Realism.** Hs perceive the world with analytical detail. They make relational decisions after gathering data based on research, previous training and experience, and current conditions. If a relationship doesn't match an H's ideals of independence and functionality, the H is likely to end it.

Meet a Typical H

Nancy is a professional woman in her thirties who is a wife and mother of two grade school-aged girls. She and her wife have been together for almost a decade. Nancy grew up not needing a lot of supervision or assistance. She made her own bed, her own lunch, and her own prom dress. She earned her own money as soon as she was legally allowed to be employed in an after-school job. She decided to settle down with her wife because she was the only long-term partner that didn't become upset if she didn't call her back for days when she was studying for tests in law school. She also appreciated that her wife could spend Christmas skiing with her friends while she traveled back to her hometown to her enjoy her grandmother's traditional Christmas celebrations.

Nancy deeply appreciates her marriage because she and her wife created a secure home life, and they do things together and apart. She and her wife have regular date nights, hike together, and consider themselves great coparents. When they decided to have children, Nancy was relieved that she could go back to work after the first month because her wife chose to stay home the second month. She secretly delighted in being able to stay home alone in the house when her wife took the kids out and was thrilled when they moved to a new house where there was room for both she and her wife to create large, comfortable separate home offices.

Nancy wouldn't assume that she should attend her wife's work gatherings, finish her sentences, or call for advice before she makes a decision. She is an extremely difficult person to buy presents for, because she typically gets what she wants for herself. Nancy may be independent, but that doesn't mean she is rude or inconsiderate. Nancy's wife would be the first person to say that Nancy is the most committed person she knows, as she always aims to be her absolute best as an individual in order to serve her family. She is simply and genuinely fulfilled when they are enjoying time together.

The H's Vision for a Relationship

"There's you, there's me, and there's us."

The H's ideal relationship is one in which both parties maintain responsibility for themselves *and* for the relationship. An H needs each partner to pull his/her own weight and put an equal amount of effort into sustaining the bridge of connection that bonds them.

Hs take commitments seriously, including their commitments to themselves. If something goes wrong, Hs will typically say, "I got this" or "You got this," depending on whose side the problem falls in. Hs don't automatically extend help unless specifically asked. They praise from afar and remind their partners that they are capable of accomplishing whatever goals they chase. Likewise, Hs set their own standards for any task they take on, and don't assume that anyone, even their partner, will share the workload They would like their partners to be responsive and give objective advice, but they don't expect to get their hands dirty in problems, challenges, or even to-do lists that don't "belong" to them. Although they may appreciate hearing what's going on that is relevant to their partners, the last thing they want to do is micromanage

If H's Love Life Had a Slogan, It Would Be...

"I want you to want me, not need me."

Listen, H, you are the type who doesn't need much. You're unassuming and skilled at taking care of yourself. Because of your grounded nature and external confidence, others often do appreciate your stability. You may find this a tricky dynamic to be caught in. You want to help your significant other, but not so much that he or she comes to depend on your help. You want to maintain a degree of emotional distance no matter how great your relationship is.

Hs in Disguise

In many cultures, putting your own needs first is labeled "selfish" and viewed as counterproductive to good relationships. Many people are Hs in disguise because they have families that value other romantic dynamics, such as compromising, shared decision making, and interdependency, more than self-reliance. Like the rest of us, Hs are bombarded daily with love songs, romantic movies, and gossip about celebrity relationships where unity, rather than independence, is the norm even though they themselves consider many old-paradigm romantic ideals unrealistic.

Consider some of the negative messages we see, read, or hear about needing independence in an intimate relationship. These messages may come from previous or current relationships, your family of origin, or yourself. Our culture often equates love with "being on the same page," which many Hs aren't comfortable with. Is there a negative message that easily comes to mind?

Hs in disguise are found across all sexual orientations, martial statuses, genders, and generations. Sometimes, they are people who unconsciously desire to be independent but enjoy sharing a strong connection with another person. They can even complain when others are too independent. I know many people who feel tremendously guilty for how good they feel when their partner is away, or even that they appear to "need less" from their significant other than other couples.

An H friend once admitted, "Sometimes I wonder if I really want to get so close and share so much with someone. where she is in a good position to hurt me." He reported that he struggled to feel comfortable with how much space he liked in a relationship, no matter how amazing his previous girlfriends were. He feared that he was psychologically "not a good fit" for marriage. He was, he just needed to understand his own code.

If Hs in disguise are trying to pretend that being self-reliant is problematic to partnering, they may be either avoiding significant relationships all together or adopting a different style in order to find or sustain the connection they desire.

Your Guide to Understanding Yourself as an H

If you are an H, then the following descriptions are likely to seem familiar. Where do you see yourself more clearly?

COMMON H ROMANTIC GESTURES

Hs like doing things for, or with, their significant others. Hs aren't the most conventionally romantic partners. They rarely send greeting cards or gush loving words. They are focused on practicality and function. They will step in and complete tasks themselves that annoy or drain their partners' energy—or will arrange for someone skilled to come and do the job. One Christmas, my boyfriend at the time, a man whom I now believe was an H, bought me a KitchenAid stand mixer. The appliance didn't arrive on time, so he gave me his printout of the purchase order. The mixer was something I wanted, but didn't need, and it was (and still is) quite functional. Although it wasn't classically romantic, I appreciated the gift. A different boyfriend might have bought me chocolates.

Think back to the shape of the letter H. Hs connect via companionship, symbolized by the horizontal line. Their gestures will involve sharing their bodies, their free time, and their hobbies with their significant others. Hs will offer and plan for quality time spent doing something that both individuals in the couple genuinely enjoy doing, such as eating a particular food and engaging in a particular style of travel or a particular type of shopping. They will genuinely appreciate hearing about their partners' interests as well, and often till take measures to enhance these, even if they don't share them with their partners. This may look like getting two tickets to a show or exhibition, purchasing a piece of equipment or gear, or arranging an activity for their partner to do with someone else or alone.

#HowHLoves

COMMON H REMARKS

If you are an H, then some of your mottos about relationships will sound like:

- "You can't change others."
- "Don't let anyone weigh you down."
- "You need someone who likes it when you do your own thing."
- "Write down the top three things you're looking for in a partner and do not accept anything less."

If someone asked your advice about love, you would underscore that true love is about partners respecting each other's individuality, being responsible for their own success and happiness, and serving a deliberate purpose.

#WhatHSays

AS AN H, YOU'RE STRONGEST WHEN...

- You have your own space.
- You respect each person's contribution to the relationship.
- You and your partner are sharing *an* activity together.

We all like situations that feel easy and effortless. If you're an H, you experience this state when you spend equal portions of your free-time as a couple and as an individual. You enjoy watching a show together, eating or exercising together, hosting a party, spending time raising children, or building a business together. Also, you like seeing that your significant other is happy, healthy, and achieving success in his or her own domain without requiring your support to get there. As an H, connectivity is strong when you can admire your partner. This happens when your partner is in his or her full, talented, independent "me" element and lets you be part of it in some way.

Allen is an H who feels most happy in his marriage of twenty-five years when he is attending one of his wife's work events. He likes to see her from the perspective of others. Outside of their relationship, she is successful, respected, and serves others. With admiration, Allen says, "She could walk away from me at any time and be absolutely fine." Allen likes that his wife chooses to be with him and he is satisfied that both of them value and respect one another's accomplishments.

Hs feel stronger when their mates want, yet don't need, their help. They love it when their partners ask for input and are genuinely receptive to considering their helpful suggestions, perceptions, and expertise. Psychologically speaking, this reinforces the need Ha have for their most intimate relationships to serve some type of prosocial, reciprocal purpose. Increasing the functionality of their mates' lives and their relationships at the same time is a big booster for Hs.

AS AN H, YOU'RE MOST VULNERABLE WHEN...

- You aren't pursuing your own goals or interests.
- Your partner isn't pursuing his or her own goals or interests.
- There is less companionship than you need for connectivity.

Times will come when we aren't feeling at our best in a relationship. A younger male friend of mine, Bob, said at a dinner together that he and his wife hadn't been out to dinner alone together for more than a year. In fact, he knew the date: It was two weeks prior to their baby arriving. As an H, he understood that he needed some alone time and he was also careful to give this free time to his wife. They had negotiated this prior to the baby being born. But when it came to private time for themselves as a couple, their plans for regular date nights quickly dissolved when confronted with parenthood. Both of them were reluctant to leave the baby with anyone else.

Understandably, the season of transition made my friend feel vulnerable. He was feeling crowded. "Now that I know my letter code is H, I understand why I'm having a more difficult time than my wife is," he said.

Hs are particularly unsettled if they can't quickly find their own solution to a problem. Psychologically speaking, Hs are quite used to figuring things out on their own, handling their problems successfully, and, in essence, being able to take care of business. If their problems become so overwhelming that they need support from someone else, Hs will feel vulnerable. Typically, they are driven to regain control. The manner in which this impulse is expressed relationally is that they will try to overly control: 1) themselves, working too hard or planning too much (which can take them away from being emotionally connected to their partners; or 2) their partners, micromanaging shared "belongings," such as the house, the kids, the vacation plans, or the combined finances.

Hs feel quite vulnerable if their significant others in some way try to stifle them or judge their need for space and independence. They will seek to control this feeling either by taking more space or by helping the other person become more comfortable in his or her independence. In the case of Bob, he reported feeling confused that his wife kept turning down his efforts to stay home with the baby every Tuesday evening. He kept suggesting that she go hang out with her friends, get a massage, or shop without to having to attend to their little one. Because she kept turning him down, he began to feel guilty that he still wanted one evening a week to play racquetball with his friends.

Although this is a situation involving a married couple, if you are an H who is building a new relationship, or in a long-term partnership, I bet you can relate. Hs don't feel good when they believe that they need more space than their partners need or are comfortable with.

When vulnerable, Hs sometimes shift into a solution-focused mode that may not feel romantic to their partners. Often the solution that fosters compatibility is to find ways to be independent while maintaining a healthy, committed connection. Ultimately Bob talked to his wife about his need for alone time and for reinstatement of weekly date nights. He took charge of scheduling them every week, alternating between stay-at-home dates, usually held in the evening after the baby was in bed, and dates that took place during the day when their baby was in a playgroup.

TIPS FOR STRENGTHENING YOUR RELATIONSHIP

As an H, whether you are currently single or attached, you need an independent identity. Here are some helpful suggestions to create more connectivity in your relationships and get that need met at the same time.

- **Remember to ask for input.** Many Hs have learned to take care of themselves and forget to ask their partners for their input before they make decisions. Hs must learn to ask their significant others deliberately for help or advice. Don't just ask to win points, ask because you want to discover other perspectives and options you haven't considered before. Saying "What do you think I should do?" about something that doesn't impact your partner at all may go a long way in making her feel significant to you emotionally. Often, Hs are given more independence when they are demonstrating a small amount of genuine reliance and vulnerability with their partner.

- **Give them another outlet.** Hs often get frustrated if their partners don't know how to be with themselves. If you feel that you'd like to focus on your own interests and goals and work but feel pulled upon by a partner who needs more from you, commit to helping him build other relationships that support him. Friendships take time to develop, and your partner may be more capable of putting in the necessary time for this with your encouragement, and sometimes participation, in his social development.

- **Initiate shared couple time.** Hs often think connectivity should happen naturally and that planning it is negative. Be the go-to person in the relationship for initiating shared activities. Practice initiating activities you know that your partner would appreciate. Hs who have the most fulfilling and thriving sense of connectivity are ones who are reaching out not only to share functional tasks and goals, but who are sharing emotional experiences and ideas.

IF YOU'RE A SINGLE H

If you're single, H, you may be getting a lot of pressure from those around you to partner up. You may be tempted to give a superficial answer to why you're single. Dig beyond your go-to response and ask yourself why: "Why am I avoiding a relationship?"

Like all of us, many Hs may think that they aren't "built for a relationship" or that they are "too independent" or don't easily trust others after a particularly bad relationship experience. If you're an H, and really want established companionship, trust that there are plenty of "fish in the sea" who can handle, and even want, your independent nature. People who say, "You're too independent," may really be saying, "I want you to want me more." This is probably something that you can relate to, right?

Now, ask yourself: "Who can help me not avoid a relationship?"

Healthy Hs not in positive, significant relationships often won't naturally seek to build them on their own. They may wait for an opportunity to come to them, failing to be proactive in building opportunity for themselves. If that's you, H, it's time to enlist the help of your trusted family or friends to find someone to love who values your independence and companionship.

If you're recently widowed or divorced, H, you may be concerned about how the end of your marriage has impacted your ability to function in a specific part of your life. For example, you may be obsessing over what the death or divorce now means in regard to your ability to parent your children or engage in family routines, or how well you are able to manage your assets and activities, or your desire (or lack of desire) for a sex life. You're likely to miss aspects of what you and your partner shared in common. Make sure that you've enlisted the advice of experts to help you make decisions that mitigate your weaknesses and emphasize what you can control.

When the opportunity arises to begin a new significant relationship, be conscious of your need for independence. An important question to consider isn't if you will lead your potential significant other but whether this individual can respect your need for space.

IF YOU'RE A PARTNERED H

Reflect again on the question above. Does your partner respect your need for independence?

If the answer is yes, that's great! Make a point of expressing your appreciation. Being the H that you are, you're probably out there doing your own thing and may not have been aware that your partner is respecting your need for space. Being respectful and being comfortable are not synonymous. Consider if your significant other values your need for independence, even if he isn't always happy or comfortable with it. Telling your partner specifically that time alone is an important need is likely to help him know if he is on the right track with you.

On the other hand, if your answer is no, you may not feel that steady right now. Recognizing this discomfort is the first step to getting to the real issue, the one that drives everything else. Some Hs believe that people don't change; that if a troubled relationship were meant to be, it would just be easier. H, this is your chance to change what love looks like for you. Take this time to figure out how you and your partner both can give you more independence and keep the connection strong. It doesn't have to be one or the other. All you have to do is reach out to your partner and ask.

#WhatLoveLooksLiketoH

Guidance If Your Partner Is an H

If you believe that your significant other is an H, here are a few helpful hints for sustaining strong connectivity.

WHEN AN H SAYS, "I'M COLD," HE REALLY MEANS...

"I'm cold."

Hs say what they mean. When Hs say something about a condition or an experience, they are mainly sharing an awareness of a fact and could be indicating that they are planning to do something themselves about it. If they intend to make a request, they will make one directly.

#WhatHSays

MISTAKES TO AVOID

Don't suggest or hint what you want or need from your H partner. Hs prefer direct requests and when people are forward with them. Your partner may get annoyed if you give her subtle cues of what you need. Hs like "take charge" attitude when it comes to you doing what you want. You don't need to be forceful, but an H *will* appreciate honest intentions to get what you want. It is highly likely that your H will collaborate with you on how to do this in the most effective manner possible.

CONNECTIVITY TIPS

Date your H. Remember Hs like companionship. But also frequently engage in hobbies or interests that fuel *you*, independent of your relationship. If you can take care of yourself (financially, emotionally, and socially) your H partner is more likely to find you attractive. Hs like knowing that their partners are satisfied and are living their independent lives to fullest. If you are happy "dancing on your own," or with other people who make you happy, this will make your H happy.

BE AWARE OF COMMON SOURCES OF CONFLICT FOR AN H

Three common triggers for conflict with Hs are:

- **When a partner loses stability and self-control.** If the partnership suddenly becomes less reliably functional, and the partner needs more and more help, an H will be triggered. She may either become less and less available, or more and more demanding that things need to change. Hs are willing to connect and attempt to repair and help their significant other out, but if they feel like the other person is not self-sufficient, is being enabled by the H, or isn't reciprocating hard work and effort, Hs are likely to give up.
- **When a partner is overly sensitive to feedback.** Hs often become insensitive if their partner reacts defensively to their efforts to be helpful. Healthy Hs are typically not conflict avoidant. In fact, many of them like to play devil's advocate or be provocative with their trusted partners. But if they believe that the conflict, initiated by themselves or by their partners, "isn't going anywhere" or serving a functional outcome, Hs will feel

unbalanced and off center. They often will regain control by leaving the argument and detaching for a time.

- **Hs need to keep their individual priorities.** Hs will get triggered if they feel that they have to appease their partner by sacrificing or compromising their established traditions (especially with their family of origin or friend group), important routines (sleep, exercise, meditation time, need to restore their inner peace when they first arrive home), or conduct in other activities. They are willing to connect with their partner when asked, as long as it doesn't infringe on something to which the H has already established a deep commitment.

Let's Go:
Bring Your Code Home

The following three exercises are designed to enhance connectivity in your significant relationships. Spending time on them will deepen your self-understanding and empower you to effectively apply what you've learned in your love life. You'll need writing materials to do them.

EXERCISE 1: TAKING A CLOSER LOOK

1. Hs naturally need independence. Name a few things you frequently do in your love life that are hidden attempts to get your primary need for independence met.

2. Name a few ways that your need for independence has boosted connectivity in your current and past relationships.

3. Name a few ways that your need for independence has impeded the connectivity in your current and past relationships.

EXERCISE 2: FEELING MORE COMPASSION

1. Reflect on a time when a partner needed you to be closer than you were truly comfortable being. How did you react? Focus on how much compassion was present for you and your significant other. To whom did you give less compassion, yourself or your partner?

2. Choose whomever you gave less compassion to in that particular situation. Write out three to four things this person's mother would say about his or her need (either for closeness or for independence). Reading these kind remarks aloud from time to time is likely to lead you to think kinder and more positive thoughts that facilitate connectivity.

EXERCISE 3: ACTING MORE COURAGEOUSLY

1. What is one step you'd like to take as soon as possible to increase connectivity in your love life?

2. What difference do you imagine taking this step could make to your current or future relationships?

3. What is something you can do right away to increase the likelihood that you will honor this decision?

For access to more info on the H, see the Resources section.

CHAPTER FIVE

LETTER A

As need mutual support in their partnerships. As naturally orient themselves to their significant others and want to care for and build security with them. They are motivated to establish interdependence in their romantic relationships. They like to do things that will help their significant others and love it when their partners turn to them in matters large and small. In love, they are highly considerate, and they want this in return. Mutual understanding of one another's needs, challenges, and hopes is one of their primary relationship aims. They need to trust that the connection in the relationship uplifts, and is beneficial, to each person.

The shape of the A demonstrates two people leaning toward one another, providing reciprocal

support. The relationship provides the most essential balance point for both, giving them stability and uplifting them. If a partner fails to consistently provide this essential support, an A loses a sense of trust. This decreases the stability of the couple's connectivity. The sense of having a shared center of balance in a loving partnership brings As immense fulfillment.

If you are an A, your letter code reveals what you need from your romantic relationship: to give and receive reinforcement. You achieve a connectivity from being able to be there for your significant other when he or she needs you. Likewise, your balance in a relationship also depends on your own trust that your significant other will support you. You want a relationship that provides you and your partner with a sense of taking care of one another. You prefer it when both people receive as much support as they give.

In addition, As seek companionship. As want to initiate quality experiences and activities together—such as planning vacations, coparenting, sharing nice meals, and doing home projects.

As need frequent input and feedback in order to sustain positive connectivity. They won't feel comfortable in relationships that force them to look after themselves for too long, especially if they feel like their efforts to connect are not being reciprocated. They are the type of individuals who genuinely need give and take, and they feel steadier in a mutually caring, thoughtful partnership.

If you're an A, you easily play the role of an authentic caretaker. You connect effortlessly by nurturing, empathizing, and being compassionate. You often see when your significant other needs help before she does, and you desire to lighten her emotional burdens. Emotionally speaking, you want a partner who is vulnerable with you and who allows you to be of assistance. You need someone who frequently provides the favor in return, too. This giving and receiving brings you peace, harmony, and meaning in life. In your mindset, relationships aren't just the "spice of life," they are the main meal.

What do As want? To create and rely on a connection to something that is more hopeful, beneficial, and protective than they have on their own. The relationship is the primary source of life balance in an A's life.

Your average A needs a relationship to be kind, gentle, nurturing, and beautiful. For the A to feel fulfilled in relationship, the A needs to feel that there are no lingering resentments or unresolvable issues. Conflict drains an A, and therefore, they often empathize with their loved one in order to get back to a peaceful state.

Some As may take their time to find a mate worthy of being vulnerable with, but once they are committed, they are highly accepting. They are unlikely to dissolve a relationship—even a negative one—without considerable justification. Their romantic nature holds a persistent hope that love will prevail in times of disconnection. Deep down, they believe that if both people keep giving to each other, they can outlast any challenging season.

As need to have a relationship that comforts them and believe that they can be helpful to their partner. They yearn for an appreciative, positive, and deeply reciprocal relationship.

Key Qualities of an A in Love

When As are in love and their relationships have high connectivity, they naturally demonstrate:

- **Kindness.** As often are at their best when their lovers are at their worst. If an A's significant other has a conflict at work and doesn't say anything about it when getting home at night, the A will intuitively shift the mood at home. Without being asked, As will run their significant other hot baths, put on a comedy show, take on more housework, or offer a sweet touch.

- **Romance.** As are the type of lovers who pay actual attention and *believe* lines said in movies, lyrics sung in songs, or sentiments printed on greeting cards. They respond affectionately when their partners validate and appreciate them with loving gestures and phrases.

- **Empathy.** As think about their partners when they aren't with them and then act on their thoughts. They will go out of their way to be friendly and pleasing to their lovers, thinking, *I want to do more.* They often understand their significant others' perspectives and are accepting. As will also make considerable effort to win over their significant others'

family and friends, feeling that this would be
supportive.

- **Accommodation.** As will drop other
priorities if their partners ask for assistance.
They will be late to meetings, turn down fun
experiences, and sacrifice their own physical
needs if they believe their partners need
them. Nothing matters more to them than
"being there" for a significant other.
- **Hope.** As tend to have hope in love itself. This
hope motivates them to be nurturing and
present for their partners.   Even during
significant conflict, As in love will envision a
positive endings. An A is rarely going to be
the partner that directly initiates a breakup,
moves out, or walks away when a partner is
demonstrating any indication of wanting
genuine resolution and harmony.

Meet A Typical A

Jack is a successful manager at a prestigious
consulting firm; he is in his early forties. Although
his days of leading his team are demanding, he
routinely takes time at the end of his lunch hour to
call his girlfriend to see how she's doing. He and his
girlfriend have been together for over twelve years.
She experienced a challenging divorce two years
prior to meeting Jack and stated early on in their

courtship that she never wanted to marry again. Jack doesn't care about a marriage certificate as much as he cares for creating a loving life together and demonstrating that he understood her perspective.

A superb listener, Jack is genuinely delighted when his girlfriend calls him in the middle of her workday to share something about what's going on. He routinely greets her with a smile and an embrace, and often returns from work with a thoughtful gift. When she enters the room, he pauses what he is doing to warmly attend to her, even if the interaction is brief.

No matter what Jack is experiencing personally, he considers how he can be there for her. For example, he felt awful when a key business meeting out of town was scheduled for the same weekend of his girlfriend's fortieth birthday party. After stewing over it for a few days, rather than miss something that meant a great deal to her and her parents, he rescheduled the meeting. Jack works hard to nurture his girlfriend.

Although most people wouldn't guess it about him, Jack loves it when his girlfriend returns his romantic energy. When his girlfriend does sweet things for him, he feels good. For example, Jack adores it when his girlfriend goes out of her way to leave a note for him, arranges a meal for him, or encourages him to take care of himself. When his girlfriend scheduled a prepaid massage for him at her favorite spa, he purchased a gift card for her to discover the next time she went there. He routinely likes to brag how his girlfriend will pick up his favorite snack, even if it isn't on the grocery list. He keeps every single note and present she has given him in the top drawer of his dresser.

Jack confessed that the secret behind their successful relationship was that his girlfriend "isn't too proud to let me help her. And she appreciates me for being emotionally sensitive to her. I'm not like that with anyone else."

The A's Vision for a Relationship

"Our life is beautiful."

The A's ideal relationship is one in which both people equally contribute. Is there more joy than sorrow? More beauty than ugliness? Although we all want to answer yes to these questions, As prioritize their efforts to cultivate a relationship that feels good. Each person can come from different backgrounds or have different political beliefs or perspectives, as long as together there is harmony. Both people need to demonstrate a willingness to help the other out and be emotionally supportive. As are highly tolerant and accepting. Deep down, they want to be validated and accepted as who they are as well. They are uncomfortable with the idea of trying to change their partner's mind or behavior and will attempt to accommodate their lover's desires more than the other codes. As believe love is the answer to any question or conflict, and often will take steps to avoid or resolve a conflict. Often, their partner won't even know that they have taken such measures. As often place another person's needs ahead of their own and believe that this is "doing the loving thing."

If A's Love Life Had a Slogan, It Would Be...

"You lift me up."

Listen A, you are the type of person whose simple truth is that you want to be loved. It's equally important to know that you *need* your partner to feel your love too. As an individual, you may be quite content doing your own thing. When it comes to love, however, you seek interdependence. Psychologists view interdependence as a set of healthy thoughts, feelings, and behaviors that people use for their mutual benefit. This is where two strong individuals love one another in a way that is vulnerable *and* comforting. Your experience is that interdependence in love enhances your life.

As in Disguise

Consider some of the negative messages we see, read, or hear regarding needing support in an intimate relationship. These messages may come from your own mind or from trusted others, social settings, or the media. Our culture often overemphasizes being independent, sometimes leading As to question their own needs. Is there a negative message that easily comes to mind?

I know many extremely successful and free-spirited individuals who are As in disguise. These As in disguise are male and female, gay and straight, married and single individuals who unconsciously want to receive support but feel that this desire is unhealthy. "I shouldn't want to be recognized for how great I am," an A friend once confessed to me. He didn't want to *want* his boyfriend to be touched that he cooked him breakfast in bed. He was upset with himself that he "cared so much" when his boyfriend didn't compliment his cooking, and the he was hurt that he didn't eat much of it. Like my friend, many As may feel judged or shamed for needing recognition and appreciation, fearing that it will be seen as a sign of weakness.

Your Guide to Understanding Yourself as an A

Let's take a closer look at the needs of an A. Do you recognize yourself in some of the following descriptions?

COMMON A ROMANTIC GESTURES

When a relationship has positive connectivity, each person in it will make overtures to sustain it. As naturally enjoy romance and will go out of the way to do something special for their significant others. They like to cook meals or gift their loved ones with feel good treats. They will share songs, movies, photos, quotes, or signs that signify something beautiful about their relationships.

As are the type of partners who will give a greeting card with underlined words or phrases on them or write out their own loving sentiments. They give small gifts regularly, each time aiming to please their significant other. "I thought you might like this" is a common phrase they employ.

As want to say yes to the requests of their partners (it drains them when they have to say no too often!) and they will often demonstrate their affection by doing favors. They will even do nice things for a partner's family and friends.

As tend to be comfortable demonstrating affection publicly. Even if an A is an introvert and doesn't like attention, he will reach out to hold his partner's hand or touch her affectionately. An A is likely to be responsive when a partner does the same.

Think back to the shape of the letter A. Given their need for companionship (symbolized by the horizontal line in the letter) As also invite their lover to share pleasant activities. They easily enjoy candlelit dinners, weekends away, walks or hikes, bike rides, cooking classes, couples' massages, and romantic picnics.

An A once brought me an entirely new stock of cold medicine at the first sign of congestion and sniffles. He made sure he brought me two bottles of each medicine, so I wouldn't run out, and even got me a children's version of a cough suppressant, because I had once told him that I didn't like the morning-after effect on me of the adult version. He asked if he could spend time with me when I was sick, just so he could take care of me. Companionship for an A, truly means "in sickness and in health."

#HowALoves

COMMON A REMARKS

As an A, some of your mottos about relationships are:

- "Treat others as you want to be treated."
- "It's not what you say, it's how you say it."
- "Don't try so hard to change him/her."
- "If you don't have anything nice to say, don't say anything at all."

If you were asked for your advice about relationships, you would likely say that true love is a byproduct of demonstrations of acceptance, understanding, and nurturance.

#WhatASays

AS AN A, YOU'RE STRONGEST WHEN...

- You can say yes to your partner's requests.
- Your partner does something kind for you.
- You and your partner do an activity together.

We all have certain experiences that bring out our strong side. As an A, you like to be needed.

Mike is an A, a part-time stay at home dad in his early thirties. He feels the best when he is assured that he helped make his wife's day better. He happily shifts plans in his day to accommodate requests and needs. He is grateful when this is reciprocated. Mike appreciates when his wife changes her schedule to accommodate his enjoyment of his favorite activities or to allow him to go away for the weekend on his own. He says, "It's all about give and take."

As enjoy the feeling of being needed most often when their mates routinely demonstrate kindness and thoughtfulness to them. As feel most connected and strong when they know that they are valued and their efforts to help their partner are appreciated. It really is the thought that counts. As don't need to be repeatedly praised for their achievements, but they do feel confident and in balance when their loved one recognizes them for their partnership efforts.

As also need shared interests and experiences with their significant others. They want to do activities together, plan trips together, and have their partner be their one of their companions. Mike and his wife often host and attend social gatherings together, participate in weekly trivia night together, and go on weekend trips together. They also share chores. For Mike, this is deeply fulfilling to have his wife support him emotionally, share the weight of home responsibilities, and also be one of his play-mates. As need to share responsibilities, projects, pleasure, travel, celebrations, and affection.

AS AN A, YOU'RE MOST VULNERABLE WHEN...

- You are taken for granted.
- You are criticized.
- You feel incapable of helping.

We all have experiences that drain us. During a dinner conversation among friends about what we all wanted from love, an A said, "Not to be taken for granted." He explained that he was recently disappointed that the girl he was dating for six months didn't seem to notice or care that the drive to her house took forty-five minutes. Another A chimed in, saying that she had decided to leave her marriage when she noticed that her ex-husband stopped saying thank you when she paid for an entire vacation.

If they believe they are being unfairly judged or criticized by their partner, As will lose a sense of balance. When we are feeling vulnerable, it is human nature to have something we naturally do to try to feel better. Typically, As are driven to seek external approval when they feel upset or their confidence has been shaken. Psychologically speaking, this is when a healthy partnership is most beneficial to them. Upon occasion, many of us dwell on our doubts, worries, or perceived inadequacies too long. If an A's partner doesn't routinely comfort him during these vulnerable periods, or is frequently harsh, an A will become less secure and satisfied. In relationship, As are willing to work for the relationship, but they are likely to shut down and retreat if discord dominates.

As are significantly sensitive if they believe they have failed to live up to their own relationship ideals—for example, being unavailable due to work obligations—and often become their own worst critics. If they feel their significant other is pointing out their errors over and over again, when they believe they have made real, good-faith efforts to please the partner, they may begin to avoid the partner to avoid the conflict, internalize their anger or hurt, and act passively aggressive.

When Kathy's husband started a new job, she understood that the first few months would be a challenging time for him. His new boss often didn't communicate his expectations upfront, leading her husband to come home well past dinners most nights and be absent without warning. The epitome of an A, Kathy tried to cheer him up, suggesting he go to the gym before he came home to blow off steam and calling him during her morning break to remind him that he had what it took to get through the hard career transition.

All of these efforts to ease his stress didn't appear to help, however. Kathy thought that taking a year off from the annual Thanksgiving dinner they hosted would make him happy—especially not having her parents visit. But he was infuriated when she told him of her plans. He had been looking forward to their tradition.

After this fight, Kathy had a hard time sleeping. She felt both infuriated at her husband for not seeing how willing she was to make this time easier for him, and also guilty that she hadn't interpreted his needs well. Her well-intentioned attempts to make things better seemed to have done the opposite, and Kathy felt uneasy about that. Kathy's belief that she lost her husband's approval, even temporarily, made her feel off balance.

When As feel like they are falling short and that they are not lifting their partners up, they are likely to be uneasy. When Kathy approached her husband the next day, telling him that the most important thing for her was to help reduce his stress, he suggested a few surprisingly simple things she could do for him. When she did them, she immediately felt better.

TIPS FOR STRENGTHENING YOUR RELATIONSHIP

Deep down, whether you are currently single or attached, as an A you want to cultivate a harmonious romantic relationship that uplifts both you and your partner. Here are some helpful suggestions to create more connectivity in your relationship.

- **Remember to look after yourself.** Natural caregivers, most As need reminders and encouragement to put themselves up front. Many As learn to take care of their partner first and forget themselves. People who truly love you will want you to feel good. Many As must consciously learn to go beyond their comfort zones to say no to others and focus on themselves. When they do, however, they are in a better position to give *more* to their significant others. Often, they are most supportive to a relationship when they have routines to do so.

- **Directly ask.** Learn how to identify what you want emotionally. Strangely, as an A, you may often sense what others need easier than your wants or needs. If you do know what you want, it's likely you struggle to ask for it directly. It probably will never come easily or naturally for you, and that's okay! When you do ask directly for what you need from a place of healthy entitlement, it will help others know how to meet your needs better. It will also help you partner save a lot of energy from trying to guess it. Practice sharing what support looks like to you and describing what you need in order to feel fulfilled and fueled to connect. As who have the most fulfilling and thriving sense of connectivity are ones who are vulnerable enough to ask for support, and to be compassionate when they say no to others.

IF YOU'RE A SINGLE A

If you're single, recently widowed, or divorced, you may feel like a fulfilling piece of your life is missing. Trust that this feeling is perfectly normal for you! For your psychological wellbeing, it is important for you to identify people and activities that do or could support you. Psychologically healthy As who are not in positive relationships don't fall apart when they on their own. They instead focus giving more to their friends and family, serve in their communities or workplaces, or seek comfort in doing activities that make them feel like they are contributing. Single As feel happier when they are mentoring, working with sick, elderly, or children, or taking care of pets.

When the opportunity arises to establish a new significant relationship, be conscious of your need for support. Finding a person who is generally receptive to receiving your support, and naturally wants to support you, is likely going to be a good fit.

IF YOU'RE A PARTNERED A

Often, As naturally give help or extend offers to care for their significant others. Ask yourself if you believe that your current partner equally is able *and* willing to support you. Although you may be tempted to analyzing or spending a lot of time to discern your response, go with your gut instinct.

Is the level of companionship in your relationship adequate for you?

If your answer is yes, that's wonderful! Sometimes our needs are less noticeable when they are being met. Being the A that you are, you probably are showering your partner with some affection and love already. Telling your partner specifically what you are grateful for is likely to boost your connectivity and reinforce the same actions from your partner.

If your answer is no, you probably feel a bit of discomfort. Stick with this clarity for a few minutes, although it may be uncomfortable. Sometimes, As believe that support should just "come naturally" to their partners. Instead of waiting for something to happen naturally, this is your opportunity to come clean with your truth—first to yourself, then with your partner. If your intention is to build connectivity, trust that your needs need to be attended to. Healthy As often try to pay close attention when something isn't working for them, acting upon it as soon as possible in order to prevent more disconnection later.

Do you equally support your partner?

Hopefully, you can answer that you are loving your significant partner in a way that works for you. Slow down and notice the connectivity you feel when you are truly there for your partner to lean on. You don't have to brag. Just pay attention to the impact your support has on your self-trust and internal balance. It is psychologically healthy for you to be confident.

If your answer is no, coming to this conclusion may hit you harder than the feeling that *you* aren't receiving the support you want. Place yourself *and* your partner in a better position by directly asking him or her to validate your answer. Many As judge themselves too harshly and may find a partner has a different perspective.

If you find that your partner truly feels like you could support her better, ask for concrete ways you could be more helpful. If your partner doesn't respond or doesn't know, keep conveying your genuine desire to support her. Make sure that your partner knows that this is a key need of yours. Ask yourself if you are still capable, willing and committed to this dynamic. Your true answers will give you the momentum you need to make decisions that will truly work for you.

Guidance If Your Partner Is an A

If you're reading this, and you think it's a safe bet that your partner is an A, here are a few helpful hints for achieving compatibility in your connectivity.

WHEN AN A SAYS, "I'M COLD," SHE REALLY MEANS...

"Please go bring me my favorite comfy sweater."

When As share something about their state of being, they often are making a request. It may not feel clear to others, but if you said this, an A would likely already be on his way to getting you something warm and comfy. It's not that As are hinting or want you to read their minds. It's that their ears are tuned to hear requests.

Over at my friend Sarah's house for dinner one night, Sarah was preparing dinner while her husband was chatting with me at the table. After we heard a loud banging sound in the kitchen, her husband called out, "Tell me if you need a hand." Sarah replied, "My hands are too slippery. I'm trying to open this jar." He immediately jumped up and said to me, "That's code for, 'Come open this jar for me.'" He knew how to decipher her language.

#WhatASays

MISTAKES TO AVOID

Don't forget to show up or recognize big events for the As in your life. As tend to see anniversaries, holidays, birthdays, weddings, birthdays, celebrations, and other shared events as bonding opportunities. As often feel that these special times are the culmination or beginning of something important for them, and they need to share them with their significant others. This suggestion is probably applicable to the other key people in their lives, too. Many As won't have expectations for you other than that you are positively physically present.

CONNECTIVITY TIPS

Frequently engage in random acts of kindness, thoughtfulness, and warmth without needing to be prompted or asked. A simple "How are you doing?" or "I'm thinking of you" goes a *long* way with an A. Dropping a note, sharing a song, offering a spontaneous back rub would be very much appreciated by an A.

BE AWARE OF COMMON SOURCES OF CONFLICT FOR AN A

Three common triggers for conflict with As are:

- **When a partner consistently criticizes or blames.** As attempt to help out as much as possible. They become upset if the partner's way of handling a conflict is overly direct, curt, and cold.

- **When a partner rejects or abruptly dismisses their offer for help or support.** After repeated rejections, As tend to withdraw and then refuse to permit their significant other to support them back. As may feel taken for granted if their lovers don't slow down to value their efforts to be there for them.

- **If they feel like a partner values other things (such as a family of origin, work goals, or leisure activities) more than them.** As need to know that they matter. They don't want or need to do everything together, but they do need to feel valued. As have a high amount of tolerance and empathy, but it truly hurts them when partners behave in ways that repeatedly indicate that they aren't a priority. As may become off balance when their partner leans away from the relationship if there is any doubt that the partner doesn't place their mutual love at the top of their list.

Let's Go:
Bring Your Code Home

The following three exercises are designed to enhance connectivity in your significant relationships. Spending time on them will deepen your self-understanding and empower you to effectively apply what you've learned in your love life. You'll need writing materials to do them.

EXERCISE 1: TAKING A CLOSER LOOK

1. As naturally need support. Name a few things you frequently do in your love life that are hidden attempts to get your primary need for support met.

2. Name a few ways that your need for giving and receiving support has boosted connectivity in your current and past relationships.

3. Name a few ways that your need for giving and receiving support has impeded the connectivity in your current and past relationships.

EXERCISE 2: FEELING MORE COMPASSION

1. Reflect on a time when a partner did not give you the support you needed. How did you react? Focus on how much compassion was present for you and your significant other. To whom did you give less compassion, yourself or your partner?

2. Choose whomever you gave less compassion to in that particular situation. Write out three to four things this person's best friend would say about his need (either to give support or to not give it). Reading these kind remarks aloud from time to time is likely to lead you to think kinder and more positive thoughts that facilitate connectivity.

EXERCISE 3: ACTING MORE COURAGEOUSLY

1. What is one step you'd like to take as soon as possible to increase connectivity in your love life?

2. What difference do you imagine taking this step could make to your current or future relationships?

3. What is something you can do right away to increase the likelihood that you will honor this decision?

For access to more info on the A, see the Resources section.

CHAPTER SIX

LETTER Y

A bove all else, if you are a Y, you need to be unified with your partner.

Ys are naturally motivated to merge their lives with those of their partners, creating shared identities that serve as the primary foundation of their lives. Ys want their partners to be their best friends, those with whom they spend the most time, and those who understand them the best. Ys thrive when their partner is their favorite person in the world. Their ideal partners are people with whom the Ys can be imperfect and still feel accepted, people whose presence makes the Ys feel like they are on a championship team.

The beauty of the letter code system is that it quickly helps us find the center of balance in a relationship. Look at the shape of the letter Y.

The shape of the letter Y is symbolic of two people standing on one spot, side by side, primarily defined by their relationship. For Ys, the center is achieved through the merging of two strong individuals into a fixed, joined force. The purpose of love is to be in the world together as a home. If one partner consistently fails to serve the team's goals first, above his own, Ys lose a sense of being stable and connected. Ys like to stand *with* their partners.

If you're a Y, your letter code shows you that you need to unite with a partner. Like the other letters, you may value a partner with a perspective, personality, and interests that differ from your own. Ys often happily partner with individuals that are quite opposite to them. What matters most to you is that you and your partner both make the choice to live a lifestyle as a "we" rather than as two "mes." You are the ultimate team-player, believing that sharing a strong, common foundation will result in more fulfillment, success, peace, and progress.

Once unity is established and prioritized, you will be able to explore your strong secondary need to have experiences in which you can lean away from your partner. Yes, you need to share a common root with your mate, but after this, you want to go out and experience life away from him. Your challenge is to fit the pursuit of your independent interests into your shared lifestyle. One of the things you likely appreciate about your time away from your partner is that it helps you value your relationship more. You may have a career or a core hobby that naturally provides for this separate experience. Any Y in love would agree with the adage "absence makes the heart grow fonder." You love going home more than going away.

If you're a Y, you are a team-player through and through. You connect easily through deeply collaborative goals, values, and decisions. You spend a lot of time getting to know your partner inside and out, and feel good when you can finish his thoughts, anticipate his reactions, and complement his weaknesses with your strengths, and vice versa. You need someone you can rely on to create a stable sense of "home" and with whom you can develop a shared purpose in life. You feel peaceful and calm when, in addition to love and affection, your relationship provides you with a sense of belonging to something bigger than you.

What do Ys want? To create and sustain a connection that reflects their commitment to their shared lifestyle. Ys don't need relationships to "balance" them emotionally. Rather, they want their relationships to ground and define them. Because of a high level of sharing, Ys tend to take their relationships seriously. Y relationships are like tattoos—for a Y to feel fulfilled in a relationship, being a couple needs to convey a higher meaning than both individuals can accomplish on their own. Once Ys are done dating and playing the field to find their significant others, they are committed to the idea of their relationships lasting a lifetime.

Your average Y needs a relationship to be highly responsive to the needs of the team (or the household). Ys need to feel that both individuals in the partnership are highly accessible, responsive, and engaged, with a mindset that is "us oriented." Like As, Ys are unlikely to dissolve a relationship once it has been firmly established. However, they are less likely than an A to tolerate it if a partner is disengaged, self-focused, or absent for too long.

The relationship must come first. Period.

For Ys, their relationships are the most meaningful part of their lives. They yearn to create highly devoted, stable, and engaged relationships.

Key Qualities of a Y in Love

When Ys are in love and their relationships have a high degree of connectivity, they naturally demonstrate:

- **Loyalty.** Ys don't make plans without considering their partners. Many will routinely ask their significant others for their input or blessing prior to leaning away. The aim is keeping the relationship safe and preventing something from occurring that might not work for the union. Ys are like watchdogs for their relationships. They are absolutely attentive and guard against outside threats.
- **Reliability.** On a normal day, if a Y's significant other calls, the Y will pick up the phone or call back within an hour. If the Y doesn't do so, his or her partner will be surprised and may even feel concerned. Ys feel secure knowing that their partners are "all good."
- **Predictability.** Ys appreciate traditions, routines, and rituals because the predictable rhythm facilitates efficiency in their team. As one Y woman I interviewed explained to me, the

importance of being home by a certain time each night is that "it would cost too much energy trying to figure it out together every day. If I am late, or he is late, one of us won't be able to sleep or really enjoy the nighttime activities we are doing alone. The schedule helps us take care of us." This doesn't mean that the Y as an individual is predictable, just that she brings this predictability to her most intimate relationship.

- **Dedication.** Ys actively devote quality time to their partners before others. They want to go where their partners go and experience life together as much as possible. They want to meet their partners' families and coworkers and to share friends. They usually appreciate it if their partners join their social circles or participate with them in their hobbies.

Meet a Typical Y

John is a vibrant, straight-shooting, larger-than-life person. When he walks into a room, everyone knows it. As an individual, he is bold, quick, and witty. He is at the top of his game as a doctor and becomes easily annoyed when other people don't value hard work. Sometimes others find him to be too blunt, unforgiving, and demanding. As a partner, however, John is deeply reliable. In fact, those that know him almost always know his wife.

Jeff still calls his wife of more than twenty-five years "my bride." He won't commit to other activities if it means being away from her more than a week.

I met John through his wife, who quickly introduced us after we became friends. It was clear from the start that being friends with her meant being friends with John. Quite different in personality, perspective, and profession, he and his wife Sarah do most things together. If Sarah enjoys it, John is involved. Sarah is his best friend, and the only person he calls during his long shifts in the hospital or when he is on a business trip. When she hurts, he hurts. When she laughs, he laughs. Sarah is also the only person who can truly change his mind about anything. He would be the first one to tell you that she "keeps me in my place."

John has demonstrated a beautiful level of concern when Sarah hasn't considered how her actions or moods impact their family. After the birth of their second child, when she started to suffer from post-partum depression, insomnia, and food allergies, he insisted that they go see a doctor together. He then followed the same suggested diet, exercise, and sleep regimen as she did and constantly nurtured her. He helped her realize how much her physical and emotional health affected the health of their family unit. Sarah often complained that his dedication was quite annoying, although appreciated. His behavior was typical for a Y spouse.

John sees his marriage to Sarah as the best accomplishment of his life. There is a lovely ritual some couples do at their weddings, the Unity Candle ritual. Each partner lights his or her individual candle, and then together the couple lights a larger candle that produces a stronger flame. John envisions his marriage as doing the same. Without his bride, he just wouldn't be himself anymore.

The Y's Vision for a Relationship

"United we stand, united we fall."

The Y's ideal relationship is one in which both partners function selflessly. A Y flourishes on solidarity. Interestingly, Ys don't expect or need equality in how much one contributes compared to the other (unlike As, where reciprocity does matter). The role the partners play and the expectations for each partner's contribution may be very different. The sense that the couple is conforming to the shared purpose and contributing to the common "pot" is what matters. Ys are willing to change themselves and do whatever it takes to serve the good of the partnership. They expect the same intense devotion from their significant others. They aren't tolerant or accepting when a significant other doesn't get on board with them. Ys believe that collaboration is the solution to any conflict and they are willing to hash it out to ensure that each person is on the same page. The loving thing is the thing both parties can get behind with their full force.

If Y's Love Life Had a Slogan, It Would Be...

"You complete me."

Listen Y, you are the type of person who wants to be fully known, fully embraced, and fully aligned with a special someone. When it comes to your life as an individual, you are likely to be known be unique and special. When it comes to your love life, you want the same: something worthy of living and defining yourself for. It's not that you aren't your own person. You are. You just believe that love isn't about you. Love is about the us and requires complete sacrifice. This is where two strong individuals love one another in a way that creates a whole new identity.

Ys in Disguise

Consider some of the negative messages you have seen, read, or heard about "two becoming one" in romantic partnership. These messages might have come from your own mind or from trusted others, your social settings, and the media. Our contemporary culture often dismisses the traditional concept of uniting your life with the life of another person, leading Ys to question their core need for unity. Is there a negative message about "becoming one" that easily comes to mind?

I know many modern, nontraditional, and not "touchy feely" people who are Ys in disguise. Julie, my best friend, begrudgingly, took the Letter Code Test and to her shock, came out as a Y. I am positive that many men and women, gay and straight, married and single—individuals who appear quite different on the surface—have strong motivations to be united in their romantic partnerships.

I and many others have discussed how, over the last several decades, the romantic ideal of becoming "one" with our partners—especially on the part of women—has been knocked off its pedestal. Many people secretly despise it when couples profess themselves to be soulmates, and yet most people continue to want to find a significant other who, as they say, "completely gets the real me." For Ys, this means finding a teammate for life who is capable and chooses to join them on every step of their life journey. Ys may not want to associate themselves with this need because they reject the old-paradigm, Hollywood, white-picket-fence version of romance between a man and a woman. These individuals embrace more of the "leaning away" side of the Y letter code, than the "let's be together" trunk that is inherent to their ultimate fulfillment.

There are many expressions of Y, and the most conscious and informed individuals tend to see a pragmatic and energetic benefit for needing to "become one." Julie pointed out that, although initially surprised by her letter code, it makes sense to her: Of developing unity with a partner, she says: "At first, it requires a lot of work. It takes effort and time to come together completely. But after a while, the investment pays off: you have more resources, more help, more security, and you have this all with someone who knows the real you, and still loves you."

Many Ys in disguise may be hesitant to admit that they need to be the most significant thing in another person's life, and that this desire is foundational to their sense of fulfillment in a relationship.

Some Ys won't ever decode themselves. They may spend a lifetime denying their most essential need for unity. After a while they give up hoping to find someone who will be their best friend, often disguising themselves as an A or a W.

Your Guide to Understanding Yourself as a Y

Sometimes, we can't see ourselves clearly. This section aims to help you recognize yourself.

COMMON Y ROMANTIC GESTURES

When people are full of love and feeling positively connected, they tend to do things to sustain the feeling. Ys love to do things *with* their partners, so many of them invite their partners to "come along" or share their interests with them. If a Y discovers something new that he loves, such as a book, a film, a store, an exercise regimen, a TV show, or a person, he will want to introduce his significant other to it as well. If he wants to go do something, a Y's immediate impulse will be to ask his partner to join him.

Ys also make gestures that remind their partners that they are united with them in some way. Ys are the type of partners who will buy meaningful jewelry—something symbolic of their feelings or an experience that has been shared. Ys want to give their partners the same sense of significance that they themselves crave. They want to find and proudly gift their significant other with symbols of their love. If jewelry isn't to the partner's liking, Ys may find some other way to symbolize their special connection. Some Ys get tattoos, others will proudly display pictures of themselves as a couple, or codesign a home together. Most are excited to find some way for the world to see that "we belong together."

#HowYLoves

Ys emphasize living and sharing a home together. They often select homes that provide ample common spaces, and yet have some places of "escape" in which they can each can retreat. One way to tell when a Y is with an A is in the way that they cohabitate. The Y wants an office, a shed, a garage, or a closet to herself—something that is just the Ys—whereas the A don't appear to really care about this.

Beyond the clear gesture of making a home with their partners, romantic gestures Ys make include creating inner security through how the finances are handled; for example, by establishing secure, joint financial accounts and making mutually owned investments (of house, land, funds, and so forth).

COMMON Y REMARKS

If you are a Y, then some of your mottos about relationships will sound like:

- "There's no 'I' in *team*."
- "Friendship is the real start to real love."
- "It's important to be on the same page."
- "It is better to be there than apart. You have to be there when it doesn't come easy."

If someone asked your advice about love, you would underscore your belief that couples should operate as units.

AS A Y, YOU'RE STRONGEST WHEN...

- You are collaborating with your partner on a project.
- Your partner considers you before making decisions that impacts you.
- You do something on your own and come back to tell your partner all about it.

We all feel strongest in certain situations. If you are a Y, this happens when you feel that someone is in your corner *right now,* was in your bed *last* night, and will be in your heart for a *lifetime.* You naturally want your partner to be your best friend. When your partner is accessible, responsive, and engaged, you feel like you have wings. And then, those wings make you want to fly—though sometimes off on your own. But only temporarily! You don't forget, however, that your strength comes only when you are certain your relationship is strong. A Y wouldn't fathom going anywhere if his partner needed him.

My Y friend Lisa sold front row tickets to the Rolling Stones when her husband got food poisoning. She has always been absolutely adamant on two requirements that any potentially serious partner of mine needs to fulfill: 1) being there for me for the duration of any sickness; and 2) meeting her to win her approval. Ys naturally are at their best when they are on a team.

If Ys sound like timid homebodies, let me put that impression to rest. Ys are entirely capable of adventuring on their own, but happiest about it if they feel their partners are well taken care of and provided for—and feeling eager for the Ys to come back.

I remember overhearing a man in his sixties say to his partner at the curb at the airport, "Even though I go, I don't ever leave you." He looked like he was flying to the moon. Although I can't be sure of his relationship encoding, hearing him swear he would be counting the minutes until they were reunited, I thought, *That's something a Y would say.*

AS A Y, YOU'RE MOST VULNERABLE WHEN...

- Your partner is away too often.
- You are away too much/too long.

- You have changed in some way, and your partner hasn't done the same.

Ys naturally want to be with their partners most of the time. When they can't be, it is unsettling for them. One Y explained to me that she felt that her husband often did things without considering the impact it had on her or their family. She didn't like how he chose this career over their needs, and she felt that him being away had become more common than him being at home. She explained that she didn't feel like he truly knew her and what she was like anymore, even after eighteen years of being together. She said, "We used to know each other inside and out." Ys will quickly lose energy and a desire to invest in a relationship if they don't feel that their partners are prioritizing them over other interests. They will be vulnerable if their significant other routinely doesn't choose an "us" mindset.

When we are feeling vulnerable, it is human nature to do something to try to feel better. When things go wrong, typically Ys reach for a sense of shared safety—which they hope to find in their partners. If the significant other becomes physically inaccessible—as might happen when he or she is having a solo adventure of his or her own, or is uncommunicative for any reason, psychologically speaking this makes Ys feel more fragile. Because Ys need unity to feel comfortable in a relationship, if separation becomes the norm, rather than the exception, they will blame the separation for their dissatisfaction, insecurity, and lack of fulfillment. This separation, which could be related to a lack of sex, quality time, shared social spheres, or professional success, contributes to them feeling dissatisfied, insecure, and unhappy.

Ys also feel quite vulnerable when the significant other stops "putting in the effort" that is needed for the couple to function in tandem as a team. They can tolerate bad behavior, their partner's own struggles and challenges, and the negativity that arises during arguments and conflicts. It's when their partner doesn't include them or stops fully participating in their lives that Ys become most vulnerable. If Ys stop believing that their partners are as passionately devoted and loyal to the "we" that they created together (or were trying to create), then the Ys lose their sense of safety and fulfillment. This places the partnership in jeopardy.

TIPS FOR STRENGTHENING YOUR RELATIONSHIP

As a Y, you want to connect your life to someone and to feel and act like you are on the same team. Here are some helpful suggestions to create more connectivity in your relationships.

- **Create a sense of belonging for yourself outside of your family.** As a Y, you thrive on team spirit. You probably spend a lot of your resources investing in your partner and other family members that you may not have a lot left over for other social relationships. This is particularly true if you still are raising children. Making it a priority to build up your own strong social capital, however, can boost your sense of fulfillment. Commit to investing in building and sustaining an intimate friendship outside of your partnership. Make sure you frequently engage with and are accessible to this friend as much as possible. If you already have a close friend, ask yourself when the last time you two had a meaningful, emotionally fulfilling interaction was. Reviving your friendships will help you feel rooted when your partner is not as available as you may desire him or her to be.

- **Add in variety.** Ys feel comfortable with routine and may not naturally want to try new things. If it has been a while since you and your partner did something new together or challenged the status quo, add in a little variation to spice things up. Surprise your partner with a spontaneous, middle-of-the-workweek date, change up where or how you celebrate a holiday, or insist on learning a new skill together. Ys who lead these new activities tend to be more fulfilled and satisfied than Ys who fail to plan for growth. If you add in a little variety from time to time, you'll be more likely to band together during seasons of transition than to grow apart.

IF YOU'RE A SINGLE Y

As a Y, if you're single, recently widowed, or divorced, you probably feel two opposing emotions. On one hand, you may feel lonely and unrooted. On the other hand, you may feel excited and free. You may feel fine "playing the field" one day, and then the next loathe the idea of dating and deny that you'll ever want to be in a significant relationship again. Understand and accept that polarized emotions are normal for you. Healthy Ys who are single don't fall apart when they on their own. They thrive by finding significance in their professions, in their families, and in strong friendships that provide them with a sense of being known and belonging to something beyond themselves. Single Ys feel happier when they are volunteering, leading social groups or movements, or are closely involved in the lives of their best friends.

When the opportunity arises to establish a new significant relationship, be conscious of your need for unity. The question won't be whether or not you are a good team player or lover to your potential partner, but whether or not this prospective partner is capable of being and desires to be a best friend and lover as the foundation of the romance.

TIPS FOR STRENGTHENING YOUR RELATIONSHIP

Is your partner a satisfying lover and best friend? Both roles are what Ys desire in their ideal partners.

If your answer is yes, you may not have noticed how fulfilled and contented you feel. (Most of the time when we are satisfied, we don't pay attention to the state.) If that's the case for you, it's time for you to spend some time listing all of the ways you feel grateful for your partnership with your Y. I recommend sharing this list with your significant other and thanking him or her for building this strong foundation with you. Name specifically what your partner does that helps you feel like together you are on a winning team. When we appreciate people, it tends to reinforce their positive behavior.

If your answer to my question about your partner being your best friend and lover is no, you are likely to feel a bit uncomfortable with the response. You may question if there's something inherently wrong with your relationship, your partner, or you. You may have been questioning this for some time. If that's the case, first consider if your ideal partnership is possible. Are you, or your partner, willing to be a satisfying lover *and* a best friend? Ask yourself and your partner directly. If one of you isn't willing to play either one of the roles now or in the future, then you need to figure out how you will get that need met. Sometimes we are willing, but not capable of playing certain roles in our lives.

Are you (or is your partner) capable of being a satisfying lover? A best friend? If one of you isn't capable, but is willing, then both of you—together— can grow in this area. There are plenty of resources out there specifically aimed to increase the capacity for both.

Married Ys in unhappy long-term partnerships sometimes hesitate to separate/divorce because they don't want to imagine what breaking up would do to themselves and their families. They fear the dissolution will somehow harm those they love. Other Ys will end their relationships quite readily, even abruptly, if they believe that their significant others have failed in their dedication.

Both behaviors—staying and leaving—can cover up a true need to feel unified. If this is where you are right now, use the challenges in your current partnership to learn more about yourself, and try new ways to get this need met both inside and outside the partnership.

Guidance If Your Partner Is a Y

Do you have solid evidence that your current partner is a Y? If so, follow these suggestions and pay attention to their impact on the connectivity between you.

WHEN A Y SAYS, "I'M COLD," HE REALLY MEANS...

"Something is wrong with our heater. We need to figure this out together."

When Ys talk about something going on with them as individuals, it is a call for action to the team to come up with a solution. The assumption is that the significant other is going to step in and start collaborating. Ys do this as well when their partners say something is not working for them.

One boyfriend I had started to look up specialists I could go and see when some routine lab routine results came back abnormal. He even called one of the practices to see how long the wait list was for an initial consultation. Now I understand that he was a Y, and my health was as important to him as his health. He didn't just want me to feel better, he wanted to be part of the process until I felt better. It turned out that I was fine.

#WhatYSays

MISTAKES TO AVOID

Notice how often you turn down your partner. If you're saying no to invitations to go with them somewhere with others, initiations for physical intimacy, or offers to do something new, eventually your Y partner is bound to feel isolated or neglected. Ys like to feel like they and their partners are "in it together" so your partner wants you to be by his side most of the time. If he has stopped asking you all together and you want to build connectivity, don't take more space or time away from the relationship. Now is the time to commit to dating, exploring your relationship and your community together.

April is a Y whose marriage was in trouble. Before agreeing to meet her friends for happy hour, buying tickets to see as art exhibition, or coming home at an unconventional time, it had long been her custom to phone her husband to ensure they were "on the same page." The couple started to experience more conflicts after her husband began to repeatedly turn down her offers to join her. April explained: "I want to have a full life with him, but these days, every time I ask, he says he isn't interested in coming along. I want to be in this world together."

In addition to not joining together with her to experience the external world, she often felt like she and her husband had become strangers in their own home. April often found herself spending most of her time in a different room than him. She felt they were stuck, saying: "It's like he wants me to be home, but doesn't want to share the day with me."

For any Y, April's situation would be emotionally unfulfilling.

CONNECTIVITY TIPS

If you'd like to please your Y partner, bring your significant other on a business trips or invite the Y into some type of work situation with you. Ask the Y to be your "wingman" and enjoy an experience together.

Other gestures a Y appreciates (and will make) include sharing updates, plans, and invitations. Ys are primarily inclusive of their lovers and only want to lean away from them after the relationship has been nourished.

BE AWARE OF COMMON SOURCES OF CONFLICT FOR A Y

Ys strive for unity and emotional togetherness. Three common triggers for conflict are:
- **When a partner consistently rejects Ys' attempts to join their lives.** Ys will always attempt to ask their partners to join them first

in an activity or experience rather than doing it independently. They may get upset if their partners make decisions to do something without similarly being invited to come along.

- **When a partner spends more time in activities that takes him or her away from the relationship than in it.** A Y may easily feel betrayed if his or her partner steps outside the relationship for fulfillment too frequently.

- **When a partner has a life-altering experience or changes and the Y feels left out of it.** The separation that is evoked by an experience that changes a person doesn't have to be intentional. And it can be remedied by making efforts to reconnect. However, the more a Y senses that his significant other feels more fulfilled *outside* of the relationship than *inside* of it, the more upset a Y will feel. On the other hand, when Ys themselves have experiences that shift their mindsets or perspectives, this can also potentially bring a significant amount of tension.

Let's Go:
Bring Your Code Home

The following three exercises are designed to enhance connectivity between you and your current or potential significant other. Spending time on them will deepen your self-understanding and empower you to effectively apply what you've learned in this chapter to your love life. You'll need writing materials to do them.

EXERCISE 1: TAKING A CLOSER LOOK

1. Ys naturally need unity, a sense "we're in this together." Name a few things you frequently do in your love life that are hidden attempts to get your primary need for unity met.

2. Name a few ways that your need to be "one team" has enhanced the connectivity in your current and past relationships.

3. Name a few ways that your need for unity has impeded the connectivity in your current and past relationships.

EXERCISE 2: FEELING MORE COMPASSION

1. Reflect on a time when a partner was not a team-player, when she repeatedly didn't want to join you or was inconsiderate of how her decisions impacted your family. How did you react? Focus on how much compassion was present for you and your significant other. To whom did you give less compassion, yourself or your partner?

2. Choose whomever you gave less compassion to in that particular situation. Write out three to four things this person's best friend would say about her need (either to join or diverge from the relationship). Reading these kind remarks aloud from time to time is likely to lead you to think kinder and more positive thoughts that facilitate connectivity.

EXERCISE 3: ACTING MORE COURAGEOUSLY

1. What is one step you'd like to take as soon as possible to increase connectivity in your love life?

2. What difference do you imagine taking this step could make to your current or future relationships?

3. What is something you can do right away to increase the likelihood that you will honor this decision?

For access to more info on the Y, see the Resources section.

CHAPTER SEVEN

LETTER W

Ws need growth first and foremost from their romantic relationships.

Ws are automatically driven toward change, as individuals, and as a couple. They need to believe that their actions contribute to the positive development of their partners, themselves, and the relationship. In love, their aim is to create a connection that facilitates them and their significant others in becoming the best possible version of themselves. They need to feel that a relationship advances both partners.

The shape of the letter W reveals the competing inner needs of the W individual. They are driven both to lean into their "other halves" and away from them. Ws need their individual growth *and* to help their partners grow. The truth is that they find stability by balancing these opposing needs. They either focus on progressing their partner/ relationship or on themselves. Their ability to pivot

between these two goals creates agility, a broad range of interests, and a sense of upward mobility.

Ws are free spirits and need openness and flexibility to feel "balanced." Doing so on their own demands a lot of energy, however. Imagine of a person standing on one leg, the other leg extended in the air, and hands reaching upward. Many variations of yoga poses come to mind. To sustain this position for even a short amount of time requires organized focus, intentional breathing, and grit. Ws inherently like this feeling this type of challenge and push for internal recalibration. In a relationship, they need to feel like their significant other will stabilize them, without forcing them in place. Trusting that their significant other is going to help them sustain their growth trend gives Ws a sense of groundedness, respite, and safety.

If your letter code is a W, this duality will be familiar to you. You achieve a sense of internal fulfillment and contentment from being able to move freely between enriching your relationship and enriching yourself. You revolve and evolve. You need companionship less than you need inspiration, permission, or the direction to grow. You probably naturally guide your significant other toward her own goals, and naturally respond positively when she stimulates you to do the same.

As a W, you alternate between stretching yourself and stretching either your partner or your relationship. On your own, however, it takes a lot of energy to fuel your pursuits. You've probably discovered that you can only reach "so far for so long." A trusting partnership often provides you the stabilization and balance that you need to reach higher. Most Ws feel most energized when their relationship provides a support structure for expansion. Although this support can take many forms, the function of the bond is to provide security and balance without slowing the W's momentum.

Like As, who are the superheroes of leaning in, if you are a W you need frequent input in order to sustain positive connectivity. You are motivated to reach out to your partner when you are feeling depleted and vulnerable, *but* also when you are feeling proud and brave. You find yourself secretly wanting your partner to do the same. You want to be that same force for your significant other.

If you're a W, you comfortably play the role of a guide. You connect easily by showing the way, pointing out necessary insights and usually by taking the lead when problems occur. Often, you may see when your partner is off his path before he does and you deeply desire to usher him in the best direction. Emotionally speaking, you want someone who doesn't take these gestures as a sign of judgment, but as a sign of assistance.

You may need someone who frequently provides you insightful counsel, too. In your heart, you believe that this bond is the main fuel for both of you to excel as individuals.

What do Ws want from love? For it to have an expansive effect. They are seeking connectivity that stabilizes, focuses, and encourages their efforts. Your average W needs a relationship to be inspiring, motivating, and a source of learning. For Ws to feel contentment in a relationship, they need to believe that it is not weighing them down. Stagnation drains Ws. They aren't afraid of conflict, but they can often underplay its impact on them. They often don't end negative relationships because they believe that change is always possible, and that their love can help their current partner grow into a better future one.

Ws *need* to have a relationship that empowers them and their significant other. They crave connectivity that both challenges them and comforts them. This can be confusing for themselves, and their partners, but Ws need both in order to be fulfilled.

Key Qualities of a W in Love

Being in love means there is an easy, positive charge connecting two people. When this occurs, Ws naturally exhibit:

- **Resilience.** Ws bounce back fairly quickly from conflict. If the relationship is floundering, they will compensate by finding ways to grow from it. Sometimes, they even enjoy conflict. To an outsider, this might appear confusing, but for Ws the drive to make progress is entirely predictable. Many Ws will approach setbacks trusting their own ability to come out on the other side of difficulties bigger, better, stronger.
- **Insight.** Ws are divergent thinkers and often highly intuitive. They see multiple options and many possibilities and enjoy sharing their perception with their partner. When a W has an "Aha" moment or learns something new, he naturally will bring that information and insight back to his partner. Ws love to give

ideas, advice, suggestions, or helpful hints. They hope that their singular learning process is insightful for their partner too.

- **Idealism.** Ws see the world through rose-colored glasses and have aspirations for every endeavor they value. Ws will seek to motivate their loved ones to "snap out of that funk," get moving, and find a way to look at reality more positively. They are deeply committed to working in the name of love, as long as love is the way to grow and doesn't impede expansion. Ws aren't patient with resting, and often push or pull at their relationships not just to get by or survive them, but also to initiate new growth.

- **Variety.** Ws often want to spice things up and add something new to the routine, the plan, the setting. They are the kind of partners who are naturally spontaneous and eager to share their enthusiasm for diverse experiences. They are free-spirited and independent, as well as highly relational and loyal. They can be dramatic and thoughtful one moment, then snort with laughter and play games the next. They like to surprise their partners and to exceed preexisting expectations and experiences.

Meet a Typical W

Beth is a divorced thirty-something engineer. She has a strong presence, with deeply held values and opinions that she doesn't mind sharing in small groups of her trusted friends. She's a lifelong learner, who reads and travels frequently, engages in multiple hobbies, and actively participates in the interests of her friends and family. Although she maintains a professional's working schedule, she also finds the time for numerous creative projects, social outings, exercise, and her partner. Since her divorce five years ago, Beth has been a serial monogamist, and at the time of this book's writing, was dating the same guy for the last year.

Beth is the type of partner who will give back the affection she receives three times over. She is very generous and affectionate. She will often go out of her way to make her boyfriend feel special and enjoys finding new ways of doing so. When her boyfriend mentioned that a coworker had never tasted Trappist beer, which is brewed by monks living in Belgium, she procured one for him to give to his colleague, even though she had never even met the guy.

If her boyfriend expresses his desire for time alone or to hang out with his buddies, Beth is happy to do her own thing. When he wants some quality time with her, she does her best to accommodate him in her busy schedule. She's flexible and open to plans changing, and often she is the one changing them. She is just as happy camping together for the weekend as she is staying in and watching movies, depending on the weather or how she and her boyfriend feel. She always has a plan B in mind, and she brings this vitality to her boyfriend's life.

Beth often needs her boyfriend to give her advice or suggestions about what may be the best option when she's making a decision. His feedback helps to focus her energy. When she is overstimulated, she reaches out, rather than in, tending to lean more heavily into her boyfriend. She wants trusted advice and her growth to be nurtured, not to be rescued. When her relationship is strong, she has a very real need to be separate at times, to own her life, thoughts, and feelings, to discover her own path, and to act upon her learning. For as much as she wants to lean into a significant other, in equal proportion she hungers to go where no one else can join her.

The W's Vision for a Relationship

"We become better together."

The W's ideal relationship is one that creates shared support to become a better human being. Ws crave upward movement in all dimensions of their existence. Their vision for a relationship is that both individuals positively and exponentially develop because they are together. Ws will leave a relationship when they believe that their presence isn't good for their partner's growth or vice versa. They also want to break up when their significant other isn't deeply devoted to learning from whatever life experience comes along. Ws want to shine and to lead lively and adventuresome lives. Above all else, they seek to optimize their potential. They thrive with partners who respect and inspire their motivations.

If W's Love Life Had a Slogan, It Would Be...

"Ain't no mountain high enough."

Listen W, your core truth is that you want to think bigger, go further, dive deeper, climb higher. In love, you want to experience this together with your partner, and guide her to do the same on her own. You want your relationship to be supportive of the positive development for both individuals. You bring curiosity, and a sense of exploration to the relationship.

Ws in Disguise

Consider some of the negative messages you have seen, read, or heard about needing another person to help you grow, especially when you want it from an intimate relationship. Your exposure to these messages may have come from your own mind or from trusted others, in social settings, or via the media. Teachers and mentors can help us grow, but should this also be our partners' responsibility? Our culture often questions the dynamic you desire most as a W, sometimes influencing you to doubt your own needs.

Is there a negative message that easily comes to mind?

Spend some time thinking about what you believe you need in love. Is that message useful to you?

Some Ws may not like to admit that they can be highly satisfied in every aspect of life at home with their significant other and still not feel "content." Many times, their partners are scared, concerned, or inconvenienced by a W's need shift their focus away from their relationship. That can be a hard pill for many Ws to swallow. To compensate, they often overly focus on leaning in, appearing more like an A.

On the other hand, Ws who have been saturated with praise for being go-getters, jet-setters, and trail blazers sometimes repress or underplay their need for intense partnership and emotional support. They can "puff up" to appear more independent or detached than they really are in relationships. Secretly, some Ws in disguise often want to be vulnerable in their partnerships. But they don't like to admit that they don't feel as energetic or capable of focus when they are not in a relationship.

Psychologically speaking, as a W it is confusing and challenging to strike a balance between being separate or being together. Often, they resolve the tension created by moving in one direction by denying or rejecting the desire to move the opposite way. It's not until Ws have a small taste of a relationship which encourages both shared growth and independent growth that they feel free. They need both togetherness and separation in equal measure in order to be fulfilled.

Your Guide to Understand Being a W

If you are a W, you may recognize yourself in some of the following descriptions.

COMMON W ROMANTIC GESTURES

We all tend to make overtures to create or sustain connectivity between us and our significant others. Ws naturally go about doing this by helping their partners "be better," "do more of what they love," or "feel more alive." Their gestures are almost always designed to optimize their partners' wellbeing.

Ws tend to be pretty good at being generous with their affection. They are highly expressive and will openly articulate what they like and don't like. Their gestures often include praise and expressing their hearts. Many times, Ws will be passionate about what they like or love and tell their partner about it repeatedly. A W who likes something will immediately want to share the experience with her significant other. If she doesn't like something, you may not hear about it. She will spontaneously want to talk (sometimes at any hour of the day, or in any setting) just to share what her experience is like, whether it is internal or external.

Ws like to gift others of the tales of their separate experiences as well. After Ws have been out and growing alone, they will bring back stories to their loved ones because they like to gift others with vicarious pleasure.

Also, Ws' gestures of love tend to be artistic. They won't just give cards, they will write their own poems and songs expressing love for their partners, give their lovers nicknames, create phrases with special meanings, take photographs commemorating their dates and relationship milestones, and make similarly creative gestures. Ws gestures often have some type of deeper meaning behind them.

Most importantly, a W will highlight what is special about the connection. Ws think of ways to make their lovers feel loved and special, so their gestures can be over the top and a story in and of themselves.

#HowWLoves

COMMON W REMARKS

- "If you love someone, you need to let him go."
- "Love doesn't weigh you down."
- "Anything is possible."
- "People change all the time."

If someone asked for your advice about love, you would convey values of freedom, possibility, and evolution. Ws often are openminded, but they believe that love is the fuel to for people to become better versions of themselves. They are true believers that people change, and that they have influence over that change. While some people emphasize that love is tolerant and accepting, when

Ws remark on love they put more emphasis on their belief that intimate relationships challenge us.

#WhatWSays

AS A W, YOU ARE STRONGEST WHEN...

- You are being challenged.
- Your partner gives you guidance.
- Your partner grows.

We all have situations that help us feel strong. Ws are at their strongest when they are in the middle of attacking a challenge and can see signs of progress toward their desired outcome. They are fueled by any indication that growth has occurred. This includes indications of growth in their romantic life. They feel most alive and whole when the partnership is helping them grow or when they believe they've influenced growth in their lover. They like it when each person serves in a role of a trusted advisor.

Remember that Ws pivot from focusing on their own goals to those of the relationship—both things done with and separately from their partners.

As a W, Ryan loved learning how to cook. He did this by joining a community group with other likeminded foodies. They learned to make a perfect soufflé, the best ravioli, and their own cheese. He was very fulfilled any time his girlfriend attended the culminating meal of the month. He beamed with pride and felt that the experience was better with her there, witnessing what he learned. Each time, he expressed that he appreciated her involvement. What made him *happier*, however, was when she started to incorporate some of his tips or new techniques into her *own* cooking. Ws are fulfilled when their partners also reap benefits from the Ws' learning.

When Ws find themselves overworked, overstimulated, or bored, they are strengthened if a partner can help ground and stabilize them. Like all letter types, Ws don't readily express their vulnerability. Often, Ws desire their significant other to be their go-to resource for direction. Ws need partners who help bring all of their many ideas into a singular focus, narrow their options and organize their actions, or encourage that the W rests their brain and body.

AS A W, YOU'RE MOST VULNERABLE WHEN...

- You are stagnant.
- You feel overstimulated.
- You are unsupported.

When we are feeling vulnerable, it is human nature to do something to try to feel better.

Psychologically speaking, because Ws focus on making improvements, they can often shift into future-oriented overdrive and miss what is happening right now. When things go wrong, they typically will feel that they need to make a change. Given these two factors, they can wear themselves out by working or thinking too hard, planning or dreaming too much. They often are vulnerable when they do not have places or habits that provide rest.

Ws are most vulnerable when they feel like their lives are stagnant and not "going anywhere." They are prone to believing that if they aren't doing anything to advance themselves, or that is special, their worth and the worthiness of their most intimate relationship is questionable. During seasons of stagnation, Ws become accomplished "escape artists." They will do almost anything to escape their true feelings and needs: escape work, escape their routine, and escape a dysfunctional relationship. This running away can be physical, but often times it is mental. Whatever the form, disengagement is not necessarily unhealthy when it is done intentionally and the rationale for it is communicated clearly. Because of their inherent need to lean away as much as they lean in, distancing themselves from their normal routines can create conditions for them to fully appreciate themselves and their partners.

Many Ws, however, don't know how to meet the simultaneous need for their own growth goals and to remain supportive of their significant other's needs. Where the escape act can fail them in the long term is in how difficult their leaning away makes it for their partners. Just because they are used to running away, and like to run away, doesn't mean this behavior is well tolerated. Ws need (and almost always deeply appreciate) when their loved ones remind them that they are missed.

Remember, Ws need their other halves to provide stability. They need their partners to ask them to "stay" and "just be." As idealists, this means staying present in the moment and focusing on the reality of a situation rather than on an idealized version of it. It means staying connected to the concrete steps that will help them achieve their desired outcomes rather than on their fantasy expectations and wishes. Their partners must be strong enough and willing to insist the Ws stay in their relationships when it is clear that it serves their best interests.

TIPS FOR STRENGTHENING YOUR RELATIONSHIP

It doesn't matter if you are single or you have been in a serious relationship for a long time. If you are a W, you will always be primed for the next opportunity. If you want to cultivate a harmonious romantic relationship that helps you and your partner grow, follow these tips.

- **Share your need to alternate.** You feel happier and more confident and capable when you intentionally find ways to move in opposite directions. Share repeatedly that you need the tension between being together and being apart and emphasize that this has nothing to do with the quality of your relationship or your partner's ability to please you. This sharing reinforces that this dynamic isn't an indicator of dysfunction. Rather, it is something that fuels your expansion.

- **Know your triggers.** Ws pivot in the other direction (toward or away from a partner) for a variety of reasons. Many of them do not indicate that anything needs to change, while others do. Make a list of common things that trigger you to pivot. Be aware of them and enhance your control by questioning if you need to pivot or need to stay where you are the next time you are triggered. Which direction would lead to more growth next time?

- **Fight overcompensation.** You may find that you overcompensate for problems in one area by overdoing things in another. Be aware of your urge to lean too far away when your significant other and you are at odds; and also be aware of your urge lean too far in when you are at odds with yourself. For example, are you spending *too* much time away from your partner or too much time together? Asking yourself this simple question can help you quickly right-size yourself without threatening to topple you.

IF YOU'RE A SINGLE W

Ws who are single, widowed, or divorced may sometimes find themselves in a balancing act between looking for some degree of intimacy and looking for some degree of autonomy. This back and forth may be quite familiar to you and it is sometimes invigorating, sometimes lonely. Healthy Ws who are single don't tip over when they are on their own. They find mentors, teachers, guides, and trusted comrades to help keep them balanced while they are growing.

For your emotional wellbeing, it is important for you to actively pursue associations with people who you can call on to hold you accountable, give you sound direction, and realistically strategize with you. In addition, building one relationship or team where you learn/grow together will help you feel fulfilled. More than likely, you'll seize the chance to act upon healthy outlets for you to grow others. Always remember to grow yourself, too.

Ws like chances to grow, and they will approach the dating process the same way. You may have energy when initially dating to expand how you see yourself, as well expand your understanding of someone else. If your true goal is to develop a significant relationship, be aware that you will be most satisfied if your prospective partner wants to be part of your growth *and* if this person is committed to constant learning as well. Date to determine if he or she is able and willing to do both.

IF YOU'RE A PARTNERED W

Many Ws haven't clearly assessed how they would want their partner to support their growth. If you feel that your needs for growth aren't being met, take the time to consider what role you have played in this before moving your focus onto your partner. Growing yourself as your partner's partner is likely to stimulate you if you're a W!

Next, consider your partner's role in your growth needs. She may be growing less on her own than you'd like her to be. If this is the case, consider if she may need to grow as much as you do. She also may not be growing the relationship or helping *you* grow as much as you'd prefer. What specific goals would you like the relationship or yourself to move toward? Be specific in naming them first on your own. Then have a conversation as a couple to decide if she *and* you are both capable and willing to grow toward them. If not, your expectations for this potential growth may be unrealistic. It's time that you find your own support outside of the partnership to help guide you on the best solution for your relationship.

Be conscious of how you automatically value growth or potential development over gratitude for current blessings. You may often find yourself constantly questioning if you and your partner are growing enough. Remember that self-inquiry may be something that you just do naturally, like how you question everything, and not a sign that you need an improvement plan. Practice doubting your doubts. This habit is likely to bring you, and your significant other, a degree of compassion and patience.

#WhatLoveLooksLiketoW

Once Clark discovered that he was a W, he immediately went home and told his wife of eighteen years, "Thank you for being so patient and understanding of my need to soul search, learn new skills and hobbies, and ask so many questions." He told her that he was sorry for he unfairly judging her for being too closed off or too slow to try new things, and that he was going to criticize her less. He also apologized for not noticing how much he appreciated it when she helped reign in his bright ideas by giving her honest, straightforward advice.

Clark reported that this conversation itself grew their connection, and that this was fulfilling for him.

Guidance If Your Partner Is a W

You may be reading this and say to yourself *That's him!* or *She always does that!* If you believe your partner is a W, try out these suggestions to enhance your connection.

WHEN A W SAYS, "I'M COLD,"
SHE REALLY MEANS...

"Look at what a badass I am for learning how to overcome conditions like these!"

Ws try to find the bright side of any situation. The fact that the situation is less than desirable may actually be fueling for her. Often, they aren't looking for their partner to do anything for them. However, if the situation keeps happening, Ws will appreciate you for asking if they'd like for some guidance on how to handle the situation.

#WhatWSays

MISTAKES TO AVOID

If a W seems to be spinning mentally and appears to be overwhelmed or ruminating on something, avoid letting him or her figure it out alone. Don't be fooled by Ws enthusiasm or willingness to work it out on their own. Although independent, Ws want a partner who can intervene and guide them directly. If your significant other rejects your intervention, don't take it as a sign that he or she doesn't need your support. Your partner probably does. Try asking if you can help provide well-intention direction another time.

CONNECTIVITY TIPS

Commit to occasionally learning something new on your own and share why it matters to you with your W. Your W will like to hear and see you grow without his involvement, but also do what he can to cheerlead, motivate, and encourage you. Ws deeply appreciate being around other people who are actively learning new things and get even more turned on when that person is you.

Make a habit of asking your W about her current goals or future vision. Although your W might have many of ideas, offer to help your partner progress in some way toward *one of them*. Even just talking about it on a routine basis may help provide her with focus and motivation.

A few months after the birth of their second child, Mark realized that he had put on thirty pounds. He joined a CrossFit gym and began to follow a specific diet regimen. He would often complain that there was too much kid-friendly food in the house. He felt having unhealthy food so accessible to him was thwarting his results. It took having several arguments with his wife to finally to admit that he was trying to lose weight. Once Mark's wife realized this, she stopped buying the foods he was likely to be tempted by. She was able to grasp how much the diet truly meant to him once she understood how to help him get the results he wanted.

BE AWARE OF COMMON SOURCES OF CONFLICT FOR A W

Ws strive for growth and empowerment. Three common triggers for conflict are:

- **When a partner, either unconsciously or with clear intent, stifles the W's growth. Ws often share only a fraction of their ideas, projects, or interests with their partner.** If they do, and they perceive that their partner is making progress more difficult for them, they are likely to get upset. The W wants his partner to understand and be interested in what happens when he is leaning away.

- **When a W leans back in and the W's partner is not interested in hearing how the time spent apart was, is only passively engaged, or seems outright distant.** Without having opportunities to lean away from the relationship, the W would feel weighed down, stifled, and imprisoned. Sensitive to the push and pull toward and away from the significant other, the W truly needs to be cheered on to go exploring alone without guilt. The W does best with a partner who isn't hurt by the W's absence and does not doubt the solidity of the relationship when the W answers the call for adventure. If the W is rejected when leaning back in, the W may feel that his or her partner is not genuinely cheering for his or her individual growth.

- **When the W's significant other rejects opportunities to grow together.** Because Ws are passionate about learning, repeated denials to learn together may stagnant a W's emotional connection. Remember, Ws need a push and pull in love, so if they feel that a relationship isn't provoking growth and they don't see signs or clearly hear professions of love, the weight of what isn't there will weigh them down. They may become tearful, angry, or feel forlorn.

Let's Go:
Bring Your Code Home

The following three exercises are designed to enhance connectivity between you and your current or potential significant other. Spending time on them will deepen your self-understanding and empower you to effectively apply what you've learned in this chapter to your love life. You'll need writing materials to do them.

EXERCISE 1: TAKING A CLOSER LOOK

1. Ws naturally need growth. Name a few things you frequently do in your love life that are hidden attempts to get your primary need for growth met.

2. Name a few ways that your need for growth has amplified the connectivity in your current and past relationships.

3. Name a few ways that your need for growth has dampened the connectivity in your current and past relationships.

EXERCISE 2: FEELING MORE COMPASSION

1. Reflect on a time when you felt stagnant in a significant relationship. How did you react? Focus on how much compassion was present for you and your significant other. To whom did you give less compassion, yourself or your partner?

2. Choose whomever you gave less compassion to at that time. Write out three to four things this person's counselor would say to provide guidance. Reading these guiding remarks aloud from time to time is likely to lead you to think kinder thoughts and feel more positively. Together, these can facilitate connectivity.

EXERCISE 3: ACTING MORE COURAGEOUSLY

1. What is one step you'd like to take as soon as possible to increase connectivity in your love life?

2. What difference do you imagine taking this step could make to your current or a future relationship?

3. What is something you can do right away to increase the likelihood that you will honor this decision?

For access to more info on the W, see the Resources section.

CHAPTER EIGHT

FREQUENTLY ASKED QUESTIONS

How does the letter code assessment compare to other personality tests I've taken?

The Letter Code Test in Chapter Three deciphers your basic framework in a romantic relationship, not yourself as an individual. It considers that we all operate differently in different contexts and is specifically designed to help you understand your key motivations in this one very specific, very intimate, and very emotionally sensitive framework. You and your partner may have similar personalities, goals, and values, but your emotional needs and what you are truly looking for in love could be quite different. The purpose here is to get to the bottom of what drives your desires, ideals, interpretations, thoughts, and actions in a romantic partnership.

How do I know if I selected my true letter—is there a way to be sure?

Now more than at any other time in history, numerous personality assessments are at our disposal that can give us information about ourselves. Think of how many surveys you've completed in your life. Speaking only for myself, I've taken quizzes to determine my spiritual gifts, aptitudes, career strengths, fashion style, and key motivations. If you have taken a lot of tests, like me, you may have become accustomed to someone else telling you who you are—you may even desire it.

The letter code you selected for yourself as you read the profiles in this book may or may not be your true letter code, just like the selections you made on a multiple-choice quiz in high school may or may not have been correct. Your confusion about your letter code could be the result of having rushed to make a choice, skipping the reflection journaling, or adopting the one that you thought sounded best for some reason. Some people choose a letter code which they think would be the *ideal* letter, the one that feels "perfect" or is the model most admired among their peers or in their community, rather than patiently doing the exercises designed to help determine the letter that best aligns with the needs of their essential self.

The essential self is the self in each of us that is free from social demands and roles, the self that comes out at the end of the day when we come home and can be real and do as we please.

Choosing the right letter code is easiest for those who take the time to listen to the voice inside them, while resisting the urge to conform to social conventions about their identities, and then by actively aligning their lives and actions to the information they discover.

Here are four suggestions for what to do if you are still questioning your letter code.

1. If you believe you may not have selected the right letter, you may be able to eliminate your confusion by going back to review each of the letter chapters thoroughly once again. You'll most likely be able to see yourself in one of the letter codes *more* than in the others (even if only slightly more).

2. Ask a highly trusted person who has also read the book to talk over the selection with you. This may help you feel more confident in your selection. Your advisor may be a friend or loved one, as long as it is someone other than your significant other.

3. Go to TheLetterCode.com to take the more comprehensive personality test you will find there. If you are the type of person who frequently is "fooling yourself," this may be the best way for you to get an honest assessment.

4. Compare your priorities. Many people resonate with two letters and exhibit characteristics of both at the same time. You always will lead with one, however. The question is, do you need independence before you can go looking for growth? Do you need unity before you can give support? And so on.

Choice is always available. You get to choose who you are and what you need out of life. You also get to choose how to love. If it becomes clear you made a mistake, then you just learned something important about yourself and your needs. Being honest with yourself is the best policy.

Review the following four descriptions to help you make a decision when your choice between two letters is too close to call. Stay away from hypotheticals as much as possible. Try to match these descriptions to something that happened recently in your current relationship, or if you are unattached, during a recent experience you've had in your love life.

- **You could be an H if:** Your primary need is independence. You like to stand on your own and you are naturally self-reliant and responsible. Connectivity is easiest when you join an equal partner who takes initiative and has an independent identity. You want to be well matched.

- **You could be an A if:** Your primary need is support. You like to be emotionally present for and to help comfort, nurture, and uplift your partner. Connectivity is easiest when you and your partner lean on one another.
- **You could be a Y if:** Your primary need is unity. You like to join together with your partner in most domains of life. Connectivity is easiest for you when you both of you are engaged and responsive to shared goals of the relationship.
- **You could be a W if:** Your primary need is growth. You like to be a catalyst for your partner's development, and for your relationship to motivate your own. Connectivity is easiest for you when both of you take initiatives to learn and develop.

Does your letter ever change throughout your life or during a relationship?

Change is always possible. It is probable that with different partners, you'll act differently, feel differently, and think differently. You might have different needs. In fact, most of us will change letters at least once, especially during major life transitions such as having a child, getting a divorce, or retiring. When we experience an unexpected trauma or loss, or expansion or growth occurs, we may find that the driving factors in our relationship shift completely. The change may be temporary or last for a long time. The point is, the only way you'll know if you have changed or your partner has changed is to take the Letter Code Test in this book or online again every so often. This is highly recommended after a big career change, a relocation, a lifestyle transition, or a significant loss or triumph.

Revisiting the reflection questions and letter codes from time to time may help reveal changes in your needs that you otherwise would be unaware of; and it may help you and your current partner to spark connectivity quickly.

What about other letters? Why are there only four? Do we really one out of have four needs?

The letter code is a hack, a shortcut to compatibility. It's a simple, easy-to-utilize system for identifying and utilizing *foundational* needs. Often, the simplest tool is the most powerful. It's my experience that keeping the code simple and clear helps focus us. You are likely to remember it easily, identify it easily, and then use it easily.

Individuals are complicated and have tons of needs and wants. Relationships are even more complex. You'll most likely see aspects of yourself in all of the letters. That said, research in the psychological sciences has solidly demonstrated that human beings have a cluster of hierarchical needs. Once our basic biological needs are met, we naturally go on to seek love and belonging. When we join together, we also have an individual need for fulfillment, which is sometimes referred to *self-esteem*. Knowing the four imperatives of the letter codes is a way to ensure that your needs for love and self-esteem will be met. If your core needs are not being met in your primary relationship, it is unlikely that your connectivity will be positive.

In an era of overstimulation and information overload, we often confuse ourselves and complicate our relationships.

The letter code reveals our go-to methods of boosting connectivity in a relationship. It is a simple way to explain why we connect at all. Of course, there are other needs people have in relationships besides the ones I've identified in this book. But remember these few primary needs and you will be more capable to find a center of gravity for yourself in your relationship.

Does having the same letter make us more compatible as a couple?

Possibly. If you are interested in helping us answer this question thoroughly and participate in some research, please go to TheLetterCode.com and sign up for our contemporary research on what drives powerful partnerships.

What is clear now: self-awareness and mutual commitment to connectivity will improve your relationship with any partner. Many individuals point to poor compatibility as the reason why the connectivity in a relationship is broken. Differences are often a source of conflict. However, sometimes differences enhance connectivity and compatibility. What is quite clear from research is that the quality of your relationship *always* starts with *you*. As individuals, we must do our own work to understand our internal drives, our own framework and patterns, and then align our thoughts and feelings and actions with our desired outcomes.

The Letter Code hopefully will help you understand why you love the way you love. It is meant to help be an honest starting place.

How can I decode my significant other's letter?

Please don't try! Most of us are tempted to figure out what makes other people tick. As you read this book, you may want to tell your best friend, a sibling, or a colleague what his or her love code is. But I hope you will exclusively focus on your own needs and take responsibility for your fulfillment. The effectiveness of this hack resides in all of us self-describing our needs in love.

Remember, we often don't show up authentically with other people. Not because we are lying, but because we feel like we should play certain roles in our social relationships. This book offers us a way to get real with ourselves first so that we can be genuine with the person we love.

When we try to do inner work for others, we propagate a culture in which self-reflection and ownership of our personal development relies on external conditions rather than on the condition of our own hearts. Please give this book to the people you love and care about. Then wait for them to find out for themselves who they are. When they come to you and share their responses, the conversation will occur from a place of self-awareness that has the potential to catalyze a genuine connection.

It's good to remember that we can never change other people. Only ourselves.

What do I do now that I know my needs?

What do you want to do?

Spending some time answering that question is likely to lead to the most helpful way ahead.

You are encouraged to start living in the truth that your needs matter. Many of us have left or been encouraged to leave a significant other who didn't meet our needs. A male friend of mine once broke up with a woman because she needed him to call her every night. He said that she couldn't go to sleep without hearing his voice. When I asked him if she had told him that was the specific reason that he had to call her each night, he said no. When I asked if he had asked her to call him, thereby putting her need in her own hands, he told me no. Eventually, he simply avoided contact with her. Maybe his girlfriend didn't need a call, maybe she only needed to feel like he was "there to support her," or maybe she needed to hear something about his day and then support him. The bottom line is: He won't know because he never asked her! And he definitely *never* asked for space to himself from time to time. He tried to quickly accommodate her need without truly understanding it and without teaching her what he needed, in order to accommodate her wishes or find a compromise.

When honoring our needs becomes routine, we are more likely to ask—not demand—that someone else also honors them. I believe this honoring accelerates our sense of compatibility. When a lover, significant other, or spouse *routinely* chooses not to participate in building a relationship where both people's needs are both clearly identified and honored, it's time to ask, "What are we doing here?"

In Germany, where I lived for a decade, my wisest friend, who is a motherlike figure to me, often says, "You can't bake a man." The idiom suggests that we shouldn't demand that all our specific needs and wants and be met by another person right here, right now. The Letter Code system gives you enough generality to point you in the right direction of connectivity, without making overly specific demands.

After guiding me, this same wise woman would always advise, "You have the choice of whether or not to have a partner in your life." This truth sets us free. We all get to choose to whom we give our hearts.

CONCLUSION

Every expert in the various fields of psychology will remind us that negativity, upsets, confrontation, and conflict are not always indications that something is wrong. These challenges can serve the partnership when both parties are actively attending to one another's needs. Perfection isn't the aim. Psychological attachment research has demonstrated over and over again that being "good enough" at meeting needs creates the most healthy and satisfying relationships.

Knowing and caring deeply about what *you* need and asking for it is pretty radical. When your partner doesn't have the capacity or the desire to be "good enough" in meeting your heartfelt needs, then please release this person back into the romantic marketplace so you may both find someone more compatible. In the field of emotional intelligence, this action requires you to be self-aware, other-aware, and relationally motivated. Do the release sooner rather than later to prevent more pain and to avoid delaying you both from living your best lives. I have needed to heed this advice countless times.

When you know, accept, and ask for your needs to be met from a state of being in which *you feel aligned* most of the time, they generally are. Sometimes they are not met immediately, but most of the time, you'll be surprised how eager others are to give when you ask with the intention to build a better connection. Emotionally speaking, we humans are hardwired to say yes to specific requests that we believe are genuine and sincere. And this is what most of us are looking for in life: joining our life with that of another person in a way that brings us fulfillment.

I wish you energy, ease, and fulfillment in your connectivity loving by your code.

THE LETTER CODE CHEAT SHEET

H **"The Sovereign"**	A **"The Caregiver"**
Needs independence. Wants a self-reliant and respectful partner as a companion. Is most balanced when grounded on his/her own.	Needs support. Wants an understanding and helpful partner as a companion. Is most balanced when both partners are giving.
W **"The Guide"**	Y **"The Best Friend"**
Needs growth. Wants a self-actualizing partner as an advisor. Is most balanced when open and anchored.	Needs unity. Wants a committed partner as a teammate. Is most balanced when both partners are grounded in the relationship.

ACKNOWLEDGMENTS

For the last four years, much of my attention has been focused on exploring the hidden dynamics of love. I have pushed, pulled, run away, balked, blamed, stayed too long, and in general over processed my own experiences. Truly, I acknowledge every crush (fleeting and sustained), every date, every love interest, and every boyfriend. You were my pilgrimage. Thank you for coming into my life, whether you intended to or not, and for being part of my growth. It is only because of you that I learned how to easily connect with the most vulnerable and victorious heart in my core.

To the ones, both romantic and platonic, who dared to love me and partner with me during the last few months of this project: May God bless your fortitude in being with me for part of this healing, real-life experiment. You were a light on and my comfort in the rain. I apologize for my intensity, my hunger to understand you, and my incessant questions and extroverted observations. I'm sure that my focus was often relentless and easily exhausting. I am ever grateful that you showed me what hurt and what helped, and covertly reminded me to live from my own truth. Thank you for contributing, in ways small and profound, in the name of love.

I am indebted to the authentic group of women I randomly encountered while hiking the W Trek in Torres del Paine two years ago. For M., I am blessed that you shared your mother/grandmother's wisdom that people are looking for different things in love. Thank you for validating my theory and planting the visual in my mind that individuals love in a similar way to how the lines of letters touch. The backpacking group formed on that trip helped me form hypotheses around Hs, As, Ys, and Ws, sparking my obsession. You all shaped my self-awareness more than I could have ever imagined.

We may not expect that those we meet along the way will transform our hearts, but we can trust that such surprises will happen.

Thank you to my group of friends, fellow leaders, my beta-dinner guests, close confidants, and other acquaintances who let me share the emerging Letter Code "classification" system with them. For those of you who listened to my theories and then shared your hearts and heads, and those who took the various tests and participated in numerous check-ins regarding my theories and findings: I love you! This is how ideas are born, sharpened, and spread. A small comment turned into several conversations, which turned into a system of thought, which turned into a theory, which my friends and colleagues then intentionally tested out *and lived* with me. **This book is a consequence of connectivity.**

To K.B., I am modestly grateful for your knack of nicknaming me. Thank you for calling me the Executive Shaman. You saw me quickly, and purely, and without expecting anything in return. This is selfless service.

To Eva Isabel Us: You took the concepts near to my heart and gave them form. Your art is an illumination. Thanks for shining.

To the mincer of words, the sharpener of voices, and the swirler of tones, my editor and personal shaman, Stephanie Gunning. You didn't just edit my words, you edited me. Thank you for doing it deliberately, authentically, and often on my own curious timetable. Simply, the world needs your soul in our shared language. I am lucky it is now in mine.

To L.S.: Yes.

Finally, I acknowledge that I would not have published this or achieved any academic or professional goal had it not been my sixth-grade teacher, Susan Mayfield. Thank you for deciphering me and changing the course of my life. When others ask me who the most influential person in my life has been, your name is my answer. It is because of you, and all beings like you, that I believe there's hope. At any point, change is always possible. I am convinced we have the power to remind those who have forgotten, *especially ourselves*, that the world is waiting on us to be who we really are. I endeavor daily, to remember.

Our lives aren't our own; our ideas and hearts are bound to one another. All my contributions are the result of the type of connectivity that leads to shared citizenship. I'm lucky to be part of your team.

VISIT MY WEBSITES

TheExecutiveShaman.com

Join myself and a group of conscious collaborators on this online platform designed to catalyze the growth of self-awareness, influence, and connectivity. I have developed a specific set of programs, resources, and offerings that will enable you to take on the life you want and lead with purpose and resilience.

Ready. *An individualized coaching program.* Most of us aren't *ready* for leading our most fulfilled and peaceful lives. Ready is a virtual and highly confidential development program aimed to increase a leader's resilience, social capital, and emotional intelligence.

Summits. *A group collaboration.* An elite online experience for a small, hand-selected cohort of like-minded leaders, where you will receive the highly experiential and individualized support necessary to intentionally change.

Executive Shaman Podcast. *A weekly strategy series.* On the *Executive Shaman Podcast,* you'll discover insights and learn models geared to restructure your core beliefs, thoughts, and behavior toward the results you want.

With over fifteen years of experience in behavioral psychology and coaching performance-driven teams, private and corporate clients can collaborate with me to change a team's culture or to enhance positive working dynamics between key partners. Visit theexecutiveshaman.com to access the expert support you need to be ready for the demanding work that thriving partnerships, teams, leadership, and organizations require.

TheLetterCode.com

Want a deeper dive into "the why" of love? Make sure you visit the book's website in order to maximize your use of *The Letter Code* in your real love life. Learn how other Hs, As, Ys, and Ws make or break their relationships, and join the conversation on what real love looks like in our real adult lives. Here you'll find free resources, such as: emotional intelligence tips when you're disconnected from your partner, special handouts with playlists, movies, quotes, and characters specific for H, A, Y, and W, and a comprehensive test to determine your letter code.

Sign up on this website to be notified of upcoming national or local appearances, seminars, and online events that aim to increase our collective connectivity.

CONNECT WITH ME VIA SOCIAL NETWORKS

LinkedIn: https://www.linkedin.com/in/krystal-white-801179109

Instagram: https://www.instagram.com/drkrystal white

INVITE ME TO TEACH AT YOUR CONFERENCE, RETREAT, OR WORKSHOP

Connectivity matters. When likeminded people gather to exchange ideas and collaborate, change is potentiated. I am available to provide key note presentations, seminars with continuing education credits, retreat curricula, or ongoing seminars in your community. To see when I might be coming to a town near you to do an event, visit my website TheExecutiveShaman.com.

ORGANIZATIONAL AND COMMUNITY LETTER CODE WORKSHOPS

I frequently travel the world to facilitate organizational and community leadership programs. Want to help members of your community learn their letter codes and enhance their compatibility with others? Reach out to me at krystal@theexecutiveshaman.com. A partnership with me might include a half day, a full day, or a multiday program designed to meet the unique needs of your organization or community. To see when I might be coming to a town near you, check out TheExecutiveShaman.com/events.

ORGANIZATIONAL DEVELOPMENT AND EFFECTIVENESS RESOURCES

Overt Resolutions Group (ORG)
OvertResolutionsGroup.com

ORG offers diverse, highly collaborative solutions for organizational and team issues that impede superior results. Their aim is to partner with leaders to develop high-performing relationships, aiming to bring three core attributes to team culture: transparency, emotional intelligence, and trust.

Spectrum Development, Inc.
SpectrumDevelopment.com

The Spectrum Development Temperament Model utilizes the language of color to represent four core temperaments. Their team offers fun and engaging training programs that help participants leverage their natural talents, preferences, and skills, develop insight and empowerment, and enhance their appreciation of differences.

RECOMMENDED READING

Intimacy and Desire by David Schnarch

The Seven Principles for Making Marriage Work by John Gottman

ABOUT THE AUTHOR

Krystal White, Ph.D., is a leadership psychologist with more than fifteen years of experience working as a change management strategist, leadership development expert, motivational speaker, and executive consultant for individuals, corporations, and communities. For over a decade, she partnered with military leaders in the medical department at Landstuhl Regional Medical Center, most recently serving as the chief of the Workforce Engagement Office. She also served as a radio personality, a podcaster, an educator, a group fitness instructor, and a cognitive performance coach.

Professionally, Dr. White specializes in developing relationally resilient, emotionally intelligent, and results-driven leaders. She continues to serve as a private consultant and organizational culture advisor to military executives. She is passionate about building collaboration within highly complex teams, and inspiring leaders to break through hidden limitations.

Dr. White received both her doctorate in clinical psychology and a master's degree in Christian leadership from Fuller Theological Seminary. She specialized in the integration of spirituality and psychology. Before that, she earned a master's degree in mind, brain, and education from Harvard University. She is a board-certified clinical psychologist and completed a medical fellowship at Madigan Army Medical Center in developmental pediatric psychology.

Dr. White currently roams the world, and permanently resides in the Pacific Northwest.

Made in the USA
Columbia, SC
05 November 2022

70500963R00107